0/00

My Grandfather's Finger

EDWARD SWIFT

My Grandfather's Finger

PHOTOGRAPHS BY LYNN LENNON

The University of Georgia Press   *Athens & London*

Published by the University of Georgia Press
Athens, Georgia 30602
© 1999 by Edward Swift
Photographs (excepting author's family photographs)
© Lynn Lennon

Designed by Sandra Strother Hudson
Set in Cycles by G & S Typesetters
Printed and bound by Maple-Vail
The paper in this book meets the guidelines for
permanence and durability of the Committee on
Production Guidelines for Book Longevity of the
Council on Library Resources.

Printed in the United States of America
03   02   01   00   99   C   5   4   3   2   1

Library of Congress Cataloging in Publication Data

Swift, Edward, 1943–
My grandfather's finger / Edward Swift ; photographs by Lynn
Lennon.
        p.   cm.
ISBN 0-8203-2100-1 (alk. paper)
1. Swift, Edward, 1943–   —Childhood and youth.
2. Authors, American—20th century—Biography.
3. Texas, East—Social life and customs.   4. Texas,
East—Biography. 5. Family—Texas, East.   I. Title.
PS3569.W483Z47   1999
813'.54—dc21   98-43406
[b]

British Library Cataloging in Publication Data available

All of the photographs in the book were taken by
Lynn Lennon except for the author's family photographs
on pages 8, 15, 18, 34, 80, 120, 148, and 166.

In memory of my grandmother

ANNA ELIZABETH GAY

and my mother

PEARL ELIZABETH

And for my aunt

EVA GAY

and my cousin

ELIZABETH ANN, called SISSIE

who helped me remember many forgotten things

Acknowledgments

"The Widow Who Lived on the Hill," "The Artist," "The Apricot Seed," "Frank's Run-in with the Law," and "My Mother and Her Beloved Half Sisters" appeared, in somewhat different form, in *Texas*, the Sunday magazine section of the *Houston Chronicle*. I would like to thank the *Texas* editors, Ken Hammond and Lindsay Heinsen and Maxine Mesinger, for their support and suggestions.

A special thanks to Elizabeth Burke of the BBC Radio for inviting me to record five chapters for broadcast and to Alan Brown for bringing my work to Elizabeth's attention. To Teresa Miller, my deepest appreciation for inviting me to the Celebration of Books in Tulsa, Oklahoma; and to Philip Hoffhines, Alan Wells, and my agent, George Nicholson, thank you for constant encouragement.

As always, I am indebted to the generosity of the late Dr. Henry Sauerwein and The Helene Wurlitzer Foundation of Northern New Mexico, which Henry created and where much of this book was written. And to Ronnie Claire Edwards, my gratitude for many years of newspaper clippings, words of encouragement, and letters of advice.

Although much of this book was written in Mexico, New Mexico, Texas, and New York, it was begun on

Ossabaw Island, Georgia, in 1977. Thank you, Sandy West, for inviting me and so many other artists to work in the solitude of your island home.

Those friends who know me and my family will wonder why my cousin Dana Pullen and her daughter Tracy have been omitted from this memoir. During my youth Dana and I saw each other only on occasions, but after the publication of *Splendora* she returned to me as a goddess and muse. She inspired "The Daughter of the Doctor and the Saint," and she has made it possible for me to finish "Miss Spellbinder's Point of View." Her life was, and Tracy's continues to be, *such stuff as dreams are made on*—but that is a long story, and perhaps I am not the one to tell it. Dana and Tracy, thank you.

My Grandfather's Finger

The Big Thicket

I WAS BORN in a small corner of East Texas that has come to be known as the Big Thicket, sometimes called the biological crossroads of America. To be technical, the Thicket is an ecotone, a transitional area between two adjacent ecological communities.

No more than a stone's throw northeast of Houston, the Thicket is an area of about two hundred square miles where the coastal plain and the timberline meet and overlap, creating a variety of soils and a climate that ranges from temperate to subtropical. It is not uncommon to find cactus growing in patches of arid sandy land that border and bisect swamps, pine savannas and hardwood forests where around fifty species of orchids have been collected and four carnivorous plants grow in abundance. It's an area of sharp contrast, not only in landscape but in the character of its inhabitants. The early settlers called it No Man's Land, a hiding place for ne'er-do-wells of all descriptions.

During the Civil War, the Thicket was a well-known refuge for pacifists and Jayhawkers, those who refused to fight for the South. It was also a haven for renegades, recluses, and religious fanatics, but today the Big Thicket is primarily known as a national biological preserve. Five separate tracts of land and several stream corridors have been set aside for recreation and

A Big Thicket pine forest

A Big Thicket meadow

A Big Thicket swamp

scientific research. No Man's Land is now overrun with bird watchers, herpetologists, and hikers. Botanists are forever collecting samples there, while old-time evangelists still preach doomsday on street corners and crossroads. It is not surprising that fishermen, hunters, and retirees have found their way to the Thicket in great numbers. Outside the biological preserve, the countryside is spotted with new homes hugging streams and rivers or clustered around man-made lakes. There's hardly a place where a car horn or a television set cannot be heard.

Unfortunately, the Thicket of my childhood no longer exists. Much of the forest has been cut down, and my grandparents, along with most of their children and closest friends, are no longer living. They were an imaginative lot, and I was most fortunate to have spent my formative years around them. They were the wildest of dreamers, and the maddest of madmen. And although they were rabid individualists, they were similarly marked with loose tongues and poetic speech. Not only did they live their lives as if they were characters springing from the pages of a book, they were front porch storytellers of the highest order. They knew instinctively how to tell as well as how to enlarge upon a story while keeping it rooted in truth. They understood that an oral story is a living thing and should grow with each telling. Furthermore, they seemed to have had no interest in writing about themselves, no need to record their imaginative ramblings on paper. That they left to another generation, a far more troubled one.

Camp Ruby

MY FIRST EIGHT YEARS were spent in a logging community called Camp Ruby. In 1925, it was established in an area of farmland that had been called Old Hope for about forty years. Now Camp Ruby is little more than a sign on the highway pointing to a cemetery and a church, but in its heyday it was quite a lively place in spite of the fact that there was only one store, Mr. Redd's commissary, around which fifteen or twenty unpainted ramshackle houses were scattered about in no apparent order. Most of the houses sat high off the ground on blocks of wood, and underneath some of them chickens were penned and fattened. Today, when I visit the place in my mind's eye, I see houses so close together that side doors open into back yards and back yards face front porches, windows stare into doors, and doors open onto porches that do not belong to them.

My cousin Sissie tells me that this description is not accurate. She says that I have no memory for the way things really were. "The houses were close," she says, "but not that close."

Perhaps she is right, but even still the houses were close enough for voices to carry through windows and walls to almost every living room, kitchen, and sleeping porch.

I have discovered that hardly anyone knows what a sleeping porch is anymore. My grandfather built one alongside our house. It was a long narrow room with about six windows and as many ironstead beds shoved one against the other. It made for cool sleeping in the summer, and with the winter sun shining through the windows the room stayed fairly warm during the day but was freezing cold at night.

When everyone came home at the same time, the sleeping porch was a very crowded place. The household consisted of my grandfather, Isaac Brown; my grandmother, Anna Elizabeth; my mother, Pearl; and her baby sister, Eva Gay. When they were home on furlough, my uncles, Frank and Elton, also joined us in our communal bedroom along with my father, who was called Big Eddie and came from the Pennsylvania Dutch country. Then there was Mother's eldest sister, Coleta. After she married and moved five miles up the road to a community called Double Branches, she frequently became homesick and would return for a night or two on the sleeping porch. Needless to say, it was very cozy.

Not every family had a sleeping porch, but almost every family did have a vegetable garden, a milk cow, a squirrel dog, a few chickens, and a dry cell battery hooked up to a radio in order to receive war news and occasionally the Grand Old Opry. We cooked on wood-burning stoves, churned our own butter, and bathed in galvanized tubs. There wasn't a drop of running water in Camp Ruby, not even in the pond at the bottom of the hill.

It seemed as though the rest of Texas had forgotten all about us. We were certainly one of the last communities to receive electricity. I can remember clearly when the Rural Electrification Administration arrived to string wire from house to house. I will

Me at Camp Ruby, mid-1940s

never forget standing in the kitchen one evening when my grandfather, quite ceremoniously, pulled a string and light from a glass bulb hanging from the ceiling illuminated the entire room. The year was either 1948 or '49, not too long before we moved.

Not everyone got electricity at the same time. Hesta Myrle Smith, the postmistress, remembers the summer of '49 very well. Her father was sick. He had a high fever and no electricity. To cool him off, the neighbors connected extension cords all the way across Camp Ruby in order to hook up an electric fan in his bedroom. "They came across the road and right on up to the house with all those extension chords, who knows how many it took."

Prior to electricity, however, we did have one modern convenience. At some point, the Texas Forest Service installed a switchboard in our living room. It was the only thing that resembled a telephone in the area, and Grandmother operated it for the purpose of summoning men to fight forest fires. She also used the switchboard for emergencies of any kind and was often calling a doctor or relaying a message in the middle of the night. The switchboard operated on a hand crank. It made a low resonant ring, and Grandmother would pick up the receiver and speak into a mouthpiece. She answered in a singing voice much like a very loud whippoorwill: "Switcher-board. Switcher-board." She could be heard all over Camp Ruby.

Soon after answering she would frantically connect wires left and right, and often she had all the plugs on her board in use at once. She loved this job. It gave her something to think about other than her own troubles, and she had many, for it was becoming quite apparent that my grandfather was slowly losing his mind and would not be able to hold down a job much longer.

Very soon the Texas Forest Service transferred us to the town of Woodville. Only Eva Gay was happy about that. For the rest of us, however, moving to the outskirts of Woodville was a difficult adjustment. In some ways, I have never quite recovered, and I don't suppose I ever will. My heart is still in Camp Ruby, and almost everyone who lived there, even briefly, will say the same thing. From time to time, I receive letters or phone calls from people who loved the place dearly. They usually make similar statements. "Don't we miss our old camp!" "It was paradise!" "Didn't we have a good time!" Almost everyone speaks of Camp Ruby in reverent tones, as if it has entered the realm of mythology, and for some of us it has. It has certainly become a dividing point in time: DCR or ACR—During Camp Ruby or After Camp Ruby. What existed Before Camp Ruby, I cannot say. Perhaps the sawmill town of Camden, which also no longer exists. It too, was deeply loved. It too, was a *real* place.

It is difficult to explain what was so wonderful about our beloved camp. I show people pictures and they say: "Oh, how bleak. Who could stand to live in a place like that?" I suppose it *was* bleak, but the people added a certain color to the unpainted houses, the rusty tin roofs, and the powder-fine sand that found its way into every room. We may have been penniless then, but we were rich in spirit—at least that's how we choose to remember ourselves and our place. If we could return to those cherished years when life ran high and a day lasted forever, we would certainly be disappointed, for the passing of time has made Camp Ruby far more wonderful than it could possibly have been. Fortunately, we cannot go back, and even if we could, who among us is daring enough to take such a risk? We do not want our good memories shattered. We prefer to remember the way we remember, knowing that our memories, though they may serve us magnificently, are not always accurate.

When I think of Camp Ruby my mind fills with images as clear as sunlight but seemingly as far away as the moon. No matter what mental picture comes to me, Mr. Redd's commissary is always there; whether in the foreground or in the distance, it dominates the scene like a fortress on the day of judgment. The commissary was the center of our universe. During storms we gathered there until the rains ceased and the strong winds died down. I remember being lifted from my bed in the dead of night and carried into a cold rain. All over the camp screen doors were slamming, babies were crying, and dogs were barking. I remember lightning, thunder, and hailstones the size of goose eggs. On rare occasions a twister would come along to suck up fish from our nearby pond, and for a while the dark skies would rain minnows, sun perch, and mudcats.

Sissie says that I am absolutely crazy, that I have neither mind nor memory.

I do not agree with her on this. I see sun perch raining from dark clouds. I see mudcats flouncing on the wet sand. I see raindrops with minnows and hailstones the size of goose eggs falling on Mr. Redd's commissary.

The commissary was our only shelter. It was a strong building, not very likely to blow over, even in the most fearsome wind, but our houses were delicate; the sand on which they rested was ever shifting. The commissary with its high ceilings and tin roof was our ark. In it we floated through many a stormy day and night sitting around a wood-burning stove or lounging on easy chairs, sofas, and rockers, soiling what had not yet been sold.

Under one roof Mr. Redd sold everything: food, beds, hardware, gasoline, dry goods. Whatever was needed, he stocked it. On stormy nights there were many slightly used mattresses lying about for babies to sleep on. I do not remember sleeping during those gatherings. I remember the smell of kerosene lamps, and pine knots burning in the stove, and the sound of hail and rain pounding the tin roof. It was as though we were sitting inside a snare drum listening to a mad drummer intent on drowning out all voices except his own. In order to be heard, it was necessary to shout.

I also remember golden light creeping into the store at dawn and the clear, blue skies that awaited us. When we left the store it was often like entering a new world: the clouds had been washed, the heavens scrubbed. Of course, the skies that awaited us were not always clear and blue, and the storms did not always end happily. On many occasions, we emerged from the commissary only to discover that fruit trees had been battered by hailstones or split by lightning bolts, outhouses had been overturned, and stove pipes had been blown to the ground and scattered like top hats. Often as not we discovered that roofs had been blown away never to be seen again, houses had fallen off their blocks smashing chickens and dogs, and windowpanes had been shattered, the glass lying all about like pieces of a broken dream.

My grandfather did not go to the commissary during storms. He bedded down on the sleeping porch and sang hymns. His voice traveled on thunder and lightning. So, in a way, he was always with us. If we could hear him, we knew he was all right. Not even Aunt Coleta, who was prone to worrying about everyone and everything, showed too much concern over her father's safety. "Something's always looked after him," she said. "I guess he's got him an angel. They say we all do. Even that little baby out in the woods has an angel."

As soon as the storms passed and the skies began to clear, Aunt Coleta hurried off to visit the secluded grave of a Mexican baby. The houses could blow away for all she cared, but not that baby's grave. She considered herself the protector of that lonely place and kept a close eye on it.

She also kept an eye on Dr. Morgan. For the longest time, he was the only doctor in Camp Ruby and not much of one at that. He was called a pill-roller. His house seemed to be a little stronger than the others, and he too did not always come to the store during storms, particularly after he lost the use of his legs. Aunt Coleta said that he was practically harmless, but Mother wasn't so sure about that. She said that the old doctor had peculiar habits and was dirty around the edges. He enjoyed sunbathing on his porch and most of the time he wore little or nothing. She said that he lived in his filthy underwear and was not the kind of person you visited with or without an invitation. "Oh, don't go near Dr. Morgan's house," she would say, "if you do you're liable to see something you have no business seeing, not in the light of day, anyway."

I never once walked passed the old doctor's house without looking for him. Mother would forcefully turn my head the other way, but that did no good. I saw him then, and I see him now: he is sunning himself on his front porch. He is wearing socks but no shoes, and his only other garment, something that resembles a lab coat, is unbuttoned all the way to Christmas.

As the story goes, Dr. Morgan and his son were given to carousing. One night they stepped out to the nearest backwoods honky-tonk, and when they returned the next morning, the doctor was unable to walk. He spent the rest of his life in a wheelchair, and no one ever found out what had happened. Mrs. Redd, who is almost a hundred today, still puzzles over the old doctor's sudden paralysis. "We knew everything about everybody," she said, "but we never found out how Dr. Morgan got so crippled up."

UNFORTUNATELY, Camp Ruby was on the verge of falling apart when I was born in 1943. I received only a taste of what that life had to offer, but it was enough to stretch my memory far back, almost to infancy. I remember my grandfather floating through our house like an apparition, pointing the stub of his missing finger toward something no one else could see. I remember fishing with him down at the pond where we caught painted turtles and mudcats. And on cold mornings I remember drinking strong tea with sugar and thick cream and wondering why other families drank coffee. I remember churning butter, watching milk turn to clabber on the stove, and looking out a window to see our cow giving birth. Her pen was practically in the yard. "Oh, my God," Grandmother screamed, "My cow's losing her insides. Don't let Eddie Jr. see this for he will never sleep a wink."

Of course, I watched it all. What child wouldn't? And of course, I slept. It was the closet that kept me awake. Mother led me to believe that I had been born in a closet. One afternoon when we were rummaging through an abandoned house I asked her where I was born. "Right here, hon," she said while opening a closet door. Suddenly, I began crying uncontrollably, and I don't think she ever understood why.

The closet, I knew, was no place to be born and no place to live, no matter what. Like our church, the clothes closets in my grandfather's house smelled of dust and mildew, old Bibles and

My father and I at Camp Ruby, 1944

hymnals left out in the rain. They smelled of cedar, cold ashes, and cobwebs.

Closets and churches have forever been linked in my mind.

We had only one church in Camp Ruby, and its saving grace was an upright piano. The keys were sticky where the ivory had come unglued, but it served its purpose well. Every child in Camp Ruby played tunes on it or just made noise. Most of us were noisemakers.

The church still stands. It's a frame building with tall windows on either side, a tin roof, and two new rooms. Recently it was painted both inside and out, but the sanctuary still reeks of salvation's sweaty armor, and the light that pours through the windows is streaked with the dust of ages.

Only a few steps from the church is a fenced-in cemetery. Long ago, only white people could be buried there. No one thought too much about that ruling until an old beloved Mexican lady, Grandma Sally Castanada, passed away. Her grave was dug outside the fence, and there she was buried. This, to Aunt Coleta's way of thinking, was a sin. "Somebody will have to pay for that," she said. "Old Sally needs to be inside the cemetery and so does that little no-name baby way out there in the woods."

There were several Mexicans living in or near Camp Ruby, but I only remember one. His name was Poncho. He visited us often and usually brought strawberries with him. The Negro community was a little more visible, more audible too. The black people lived down the railroad tracks in what was called the Barrel House because it was round, or practically round. At night you could hear the black loggers singing spirituals or laughing, and on weekends they sometimes got drunk, like everybody else, and raised sand. "They are nothing but *people*," Mother said in their defense. "They are just like the rest of us."

One of the Negroes was called Wompus Cat. He was given this name because he was afraid of cats of all sizes, even kittens. In fact, he was terrified of them. But that's about all he was afraid of, and because of that, coupled with his love for Camp Ruby, everyone said, "It would take a cat to run him out of town."

His job was cleaning the outhouses so he was often seen with a shovel and a little cart. During Halloween some of the boys in the camp would invariably steal his cart and turn it upside down on the porch of Mr. Redd's store. Worst of all they would overturn the outhouses. But Wompus Cat said that he got back at all of the boys who turned the outhouses over because it took every boy in Camp Ruby to turn them up again.

Mother said that every time she sat down to do her job Wompus Cat came along, opened up a little door on the back of the privy, and started shoveling. She was terrified of him and so was Eva Gay, the most discontented member of our family at that time. She was constantly longing for life in the town of Woodville, or any town that had indoor plumbing—not unlike Chekhov's sisters longing for Moscow, Moscow, Moscow.

At one point, operating on a high level of discontent, Eva Gay took a hacksaw and sawed the posts off her ironstead bed. She said that she wanted it to look just like a Hollywood bed. About that time, she also moved out of the sleeping porch.

Today, she remembers Camp Ruby with a little more affection and can reel off a cast of characters that includes a mentally retarded boy who enjoyed tormenting her. His name was Phineas, but everyone called him Peggy, and he fixed on Eva Gay right away. "He peed on my legs every chance he got," she remembers. "I couldn't wait to get away from there. I didn't ever want to see that place again." And who could blame her?

Grandmother didn't much care for Peggy either, but she did love talking about him. Many times she told me that he was larger in the private parts than anybody needed to be and that he enjoyed exposing himself, especially to a group of ladies sitting on a porch. "Cups and saucers would fly," she said, "when Peggy dropped his pants."

The boys in Camp Ruby were always up to something. They were keen on turning over outhouses, or hiding Wompus Cat's shovels, or chasing him down the railroad tracks with a screaming cat in a feed sack. They tormented Eva Gay with wolf whistles, and if they weren't stealing something from Mr. Redd's store, they were encouraging Peggy to show himself off. Only once, that I know of, did they pick on Aunt Gersey.

Aunt Gersey was everybody's aunt, whether related or not. She had a sister, Clemmy, who lived in the family house outside Camp Ruby, but Gersey lived inside the camp for a short time and was a fastidious housekeeper. Her yard was always raked, her floors were spotless, her windows were washed, and her porch was scrubbed every morning. Then one day some of the braver boys went into the swamp and shot an alligator. As a joke they dragged the carcass up to the camp and left it to bleed all over Aunt Gersey's porch. It was a mess that took her a long time to clean up, and as a result she left Camp Ruby and said she wasn't sorry of it.

Years later when I came to know her, she was living with her sister Clemmy just outside the Livingston city limits, and she was still talking about the alligator as if it had been left on her porch that morning. By then the sisters had settled into a routine: they

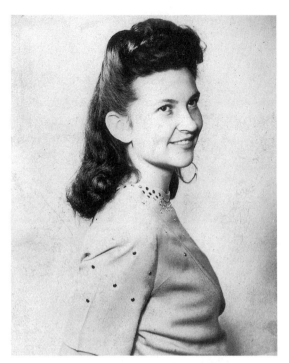

Eva Gay, 1940s

gardened in the cool of the mornings, entertained visitors in the afternoons, and every Saturday they called a taxi to take them to the beauty parlor. After a wash and set, Gersey went home, but Clemmy went out to visit their old family house ten or fifteen miles away. No one was living there, but she visited the house anyway just to rake the yard and air out the rooms. She had a boyfriend who drove her out and brought her back, and he also took her dancing every Saturday night. She was crazy about him, and then one day toward the end of Clemmy's life, he up and shot himself. "Suicide," it was said, but Aunt Clemmy disagreed. "I don't believe he did it to himself," she said. "Somebody must have helped him."

We were always hearing about murders or attempted murder over near Saratoga, the most remote area of the Big Thicket. But during my day there were no murders in Camp Ruby that anybody knew of. According to Mother, however, we came pretty close to it once. It seems that Grandfather had quite a bad temper, and on rare occasions he took leave of his senses. I never witnessed his violent streak myself, but Mother talked about a time when he took a pine knot out of the woodpile and beat one of the sawmill workers over the head until the blood gushed. "Daddy was a good and honest man," Mother said. "He had to of been because the man he nearly beat to death didn't hold it against him, but I have never in my life seen so much blood, not even on Gersey's porch."

IT SEEMED as though all the misfits in the world lived or passed through Camp Ruby. My grandfather, who was a foreman for the logging company, was drawn to anyone with a certain wild-eyed look, and if at all possible he put them to work. Hardy Cain was one of the workers. He did not live in Camp Ruby but fairly close by, and although he had not yet discovered that place and state of bliss he would later call Rapture's Heights, he was already studying the stars and drawing up plans for a scaffold to the sky.

Maynard Davis was cut from the same block. His head was always in the clouds, but unlike Hardy he was a bachelor, reclusive and deeply tormented. He lived quite a distance from the camp, but he was in and out of the commissary as if he were one of God's messengers traveling on urgent business. During one period he was prone to wetting his pants, at least that's what I was told at the time. "I'm in my *family way* today," he would announce to everyone he met, as if that explained why his pants were soaked. Oddly enough, Mother was not afraid of him and neither was Eva Gay. Aunt Coleta, who married into Maynard's clan, said that he was a little bit touched but only when his *family way* was bothering him. "You don't need to be afraid of Maynard," she would tell us children, "but you sure do need to be afraid of poor old Jesus."

Everybody was afraid of Jesus.

There was a stovepipe hole in our living room ceiling and Aunt Coleta told us children that a red-headed Jesus was going to come floating down out of that dark hole and carry us away if we didn't behave ourselves. She also said that the Devil, sitting way up high in a tree, was watching our every move. "Just because you don't see his long tail doesn't mean that he's not the Devil," she said. "Sometimes the Devil wears disguises and so does old Jesus. Both of them may come to our door at any time of the day or night,

Aunt Gersey (left) and Aunt Clemmy

just to see what we're doing. The Devil wants us to be bad, but old Jesus wants us to be good. He gave up his life on the cross to teach us all a lesson."

Although we were never what you would call regular church-goers, we had several pictures of Jesus in our house. If He wasn't bleeding from the cross, He was walking on water, and His eyes were painted in such a way that they followed you everywhere. Most of our Jesus pictures were purchased at traveling carnivals that occasionally invaded our little haven. The carnivals would arrive without warning. An all-purpose tent would go up, and in it we would watch silent films, movies from Hollywood, or we would hear an evangelist preach on the millennium, the significance of the Last Supper, or the apocalyptic visions of St. John in the Book of Revelation. On the spur of the moment, a revival tent might suddenly be transformed into a skating rink, if that's what the people wanted, but most of the time the tents were for movies, preaching, or sideshow amusements where prizes could be won by throwing balls or looping loops. Somewhere near the entrance tickets were sold, or a collection plate was prominently displayed, and always there was a table of religious prints, glass vases, and chalk figurines presided over by carnival girls who also told fortunes and would gladly dance around for a fine price. They were exotic creatures who might have stepped out of the Arabian Nights for all we knew, and my grandfather spent a good deal of money on them—or so I've been told.

Sometimes there were midgets hawking the trinkets, or preaching, or turning backward flips, anything to make a nickel, and there were always a few bearded men with split fingernails, tattoos, stale breath, and wandering eyes. Aunt Coleta said they were gypsies, all of them, and they would carry away any little child they could get their hands on. Mother said she didn't know if they were gypsies or not, but she did know that they were the scum of the earth. She said they jacked up their prices something awful, but in spite of how she felt, she refused to stay home when a carnival came to town. Occasionally, she bought a trinket from one of the painted girls. Once she bought a plaster statue of Jesus on the cross, and before we made it back home I had broken off one of His arms. For the next few days I entertained myself by burying the one-armed Jesus and digging Him up again.

"Eddie Jr.," Aunt Coleta asked, "Why do you keep digging up poor old Jesus?"

"Because I like burying him," I answered. It seems as though I have been burying Jesus ever since.

RUBY AND CARL VINSON were among the first couples to move to Camp Ruby when the area was still being called Old Hope. Carl was a logger, and Aunt Ruby was Mr. Redd's first customer. He said she was the first pretty thing that walked into his store and since the new community needed a new name, he decided to call it Camp Ruby. The name stuck.

Like Gersey and Clemmy, Ruby Vinson was called "aunt" by almost everyone. In Aunt Ruby's case, every family claimed her because she served as a midwife and delivered hundreds of babies. She had absolutely no experience as a midwife, but after Dr. Morgan lost the use of his legs, another doctor, by the name of Burr Handley, came along and asked her to assist him, so she did. "I just learned as I went along," she said. "If I didn't drop a baby on its head I thought I was doing all right."

Every day Aunt Ruby baked something, and at least once a week she would whip up her specialty, Red Earth Cake. Baking in a wood-burning stove, the cake gave off a strong aroma of coffee, chocolate, butter, and pure vanilla extract, a mixture of ingredients I will always associate with Camp Ruby. Even today, after our beloved old camp has been disbanded for more than forty years, the summer air is still redolent of Aunt Ruby's cake. It is as if the ingredients have seeped into the earth to wait for the hot sun to work its baking magic.

AUNT RUBY'S RED EARTH CAKE

½ cup butter
1 ½ cups sugar
2 eggs
1 teaspoon soda
1 cup buttermilk
1 teaspoon vanilla
¼ teaspoon salt
3 tablespoons cocoa
3 or more tablespoons strong coffee
2 cups flour

Cream butter and sugar. Add eggs and vanilla. Mix cocoa and coffee together. Combine soda and buttermilk. Blend salt and flour. Mix all together. Bake at 350 degrees for about an hour.

RED EARTH CAKE ICING

1 box powdered sugar
¼ pound butter
3 tablespoons cocoa

1 teaspoon vanilla

2 tablespoons or more of coffee

A drop of red coloring

Mix together and spread on cooled cake.

The slightest reminder of Red Earth Cake sends my thoughts racing back to Camp Ruby. I see the long, narrow boarding house followed by a string of one-room dwellings all connected by common porches and stretched out across the sandy hill like a train without tracks to run on. But when I look at photographs of the place, I see that the houses were not grouped together in such lyrical arrangements. The chinaberry trees were not shaped like perfect umbrellas, and the hounds were not on verge of starvation. I am always surprised to see that the pond was not as close to Grandfather's house as I remember, and the hill, on which the houses rested, was not nearly so steep or sandy as it is, still, in my mind.

One of the things I remember most clearly, however, is a sea of mattresses baking under the hot sun, and here Cousin Sissie assures me that my mind is, for once, functioning properly.

Every spring, as if something in the air told the women, "Today is the day for sunning your beds," they dragged their mattresses into the yard and leaned them against trees and fences, or lay them across sawhorses, or spread them out on patches of grass. Before midday the air was saturated with the clean smell of ticking and sun-baked cotton. If the skies were clear the mattresses might be left out of doors for a day and a night, but on the second day they would be brought inside again, and suddenly the camp would seem bare, stripped to the bone. In less than two days those mattresses became engraved in our minds, and after they were carried inside, it took time to adjust to the emptiness.

Today, it is the same. When I return to Camp Ruby, I see not what is there but what I remember. Where our houses once stood there is nothing but trees and bushes. Not even Mr. Redd's commissary is standing. Long after he went out of business the commissary caught fire and burned to the ground. Many of the houses rotted, and many were torn down to be rebuilt elsewhere.

In 1950, we moved to Woodville. There our house was constructed from lumber taken from some of those old Camp Ruby homes. Grandmother could walk through our rooms and say: "These boards came from the Overstreet house. These boards came from Lily Bank's living room. These, these and these came from Spot Stringer, Rosy Knight, and Ruby Vinson." How she recognized them was a mystery.

It was much the same for other families. When we moved we carried Camp Ruby with us and not only in our minds; the very walls of our new houses spoke of that beloved place where today there's hardly a reminder of the lively community that once thrived there. Directly across a farm-to-market road from the site of Mr. Redd's commissary there is now a hiker's trail, a creation of the Big Thicket National Preserve, and only a few steps away, where carnival tents once sprouted overnight and dancing girls sold chalk Jesuses, there is a forest of pine and hardwood. Here and there a domestic flower shows its face, usually a larkspur or a lily, but for the most part the hat pin plant and grass pink orchid have taken over. The pitcher plant and the sundew can also be found scattered about, and there's even a chinaberry tree that's still living, but only just. Sadly, the old pond has dried

Hat pin plant, Big Thicket

up, and the railroad tracks, on which logs were transported to the sawmill in Camden, were removed years ago. But the Baptist church will always be there and so will the cemetery. Now there is a fairly new fence surrounding it, and this time it includes Grandma Castanada along with the rest of God's children.

Grandfather Isaac Brown

MY GRANDFATHER was a man of God on one hand, a gospel singer with a high tenor voice, and on the other, an addict of Creo-Mulsion, an old-time cough remedy the ingredients of which were extremely questionable, especially since Grandfather died in a state of sublime hallucination.

While he was at himself, he spent most of his time in the woods supervising a team of log cutters. In that day and time a forest was never clear cut. Only a few trees were cut and the rest were allowed to grow. After cutting only the marked timber, the loggers would then move on to another location and cut a few trees there before moving on again. It was something of a nomadic life that seemed to suit my grandfather just fine.

I can't say that he was reticent, not exactly, but when he wasn't singing he hardly uttered a word to anyone, except himself. I remember him saying only two sentences, both of them directed to me. "Look out for that snake" was one. The snake was already dead, flattened by a log truck, but Grandfather, what with his poor eyesight, had no way of knowing that. The other thing he said was, "Nowadays, a man's got to get himself a good education, I don't care how much it costs. If he don't he'll turn out like me."

But turning out like Grandfather wouldn't be so bad. He was a handsome man with a generous heart. He created jobs during a time when there were few jobs to be had, and he rode a black stallion with a white star on its forehead. All the ladies called him a fine catch, in spite of the fact that no one—not even my grandmother—was very comfortable in his presence. He was tall and gaunt with jet-black hair, a dark complexion, and glassy eyes focused on the far away. Some people said, "That's just Isaac. He's always straddled two worlds." Others said that he was behaving under the influence of cough medicine combined with bourbon whisky and gospel music. This was a favorite song:

> This world is not my home, I'm just a-passing through.
> My treasures are laid up somewhere beyond the blue.
> The angels beckon me to Heaven's open door,
> And I can't feel at home in this world any more.

Grandfather loved this old song, especially toward the end of his life. He sang it anywhere and everywhere. Suddenly in the middle of the woods, in the middle of the night, or in the middle of dinner something would come over him and he'd be possessed to sing. Gospel music was in his heart, but I don't remember him ever going to church. I don't believe he was much interested in church, only church music chased with cough medicine and whisky. That combination of intoxicants really got him going and may have caused the accident we continue to discuss at family gatherings.

The accident happened one day in the early 1930s. Grandfather was hacking his way through the Thicket with a machete when he *accidentally* cut off the first finger of his left hand. It was a clean cut. The knife sliced right through the second knuckle, and Grandfather swore that he suffered no pain. Cousin Clinton was with him at the time, but he did not witness the accident, only the result of it, and to this day no one knows exactly what happened. As far as I know, Grandfather never offered much of an explanation, but Aunt Coleta always said, "Daddy fell down on his knife, *I guess.*"

One thing is certain: Grandfather came home with the severed finger in his pocket, and Aunt Coleta pickled it in a little green jar that she insisted upon calling a bottle.

For years Grandmother kept the preserved finger in her kitchen cupboard, and when we moved to Woodville she left the finger behind. After we were gone, Aunt Coleta went rummaging through our empty house to make sure we had not forgotten anything. In the cupboard she found the finger and took it home. Some years later, she said to me, "I just don't know why Mama left Daddy's ole finger behind. I couldn't leave it there all by itself. It didn't seem right somehow."

For many years Aunt Coleta kept Grandfather's finger in her bathroom behind a stack of towels, and there it stayed until she needed it to discipline her two children, her nieces and nephews, or anybody else's children who were in her way. All day long kids were running in and out of her house. There wasn't a child in the area who didn't love her. She was an adult, but she was also one of us.

Not only did she entertain us with scary stories, she was something of a spook herself. She wore store-bought glasses that magnified her eyes to an ungodly size. Her complexion was quite dark due to our Indian blood, and her arms and hands were covered with white pigmentation spots. Her front teeth were then edged in gold. Her hair was rarely combed, and, like her father, she seemed to be in touch with the unseen world. She was always telling us about a wild man, naked as a jaybird, who roamed

Grandfather Brown, before he lost his finger

the Big Thicket screaming like a woman with her head cut off. "How does a woman with her head cut off sound when she screams, Aunt Coleta?" we would ask, and she would throw back her head to let out a blood-curdling scream that could be heard a mile away.

There were days when Aunt Coleta had no time to fool around with us kids, and on those days she ran us off with Grandfather's pickled finger. "If you children don't behave and get out of my way, I'll get Daddy's ole finger after you," she would say. "No!" we would scream, "don't get the finger! Aunt Coleta, whatever you do, don't get the finger!" Then Aunt Coleta would threaten us further, "Yes sir, Daddy's ole finger's about to crawl out of that bottle and get you if you don't be good." And again we would scream with a mixture of terror and delight until finally she would go into the bathroom and return with the green bottle in her hands. Waving the bottle over her head she would chase us through the house and down the dirt roads and lanes. "Bloody Bones is about to get the bad little children!" she'd scream, and we would run for our lives.

Aunt Coleta was a good runner, and she usually caught one of us. She would hold her captive to the hot sand and press the cold green jar against his neck. "Bloody bones has got you," she'd say in a quivering voice. "I guess you'll remember to be good from now on. And if you don't I'll put Daddy's old bloody finger on you again." We lived in terror that she would actually take the finger out of the bottle and touch us with it, but that she never did.

"What are you going to do with that finger?" everyone wanted to know.

"Bury it with Daddy when he goes, I guess." That was her only answer.

Old-style logging techniques, Big Thicket

The hallway of Aunt Coleta's house

But in 1952, when Grandfather died, Aunt Coleta could not bring herself to part with his finger. A few days after the funeral, however, she had second thoughts. She returned to the cemetery, and with her bare hands she scratched a hole about two feet deep and buried the green jar directly over Grandfather's head. But that didn't satisfy her either, and within a few days she went back to the graveyard and dug the finger up. Without explaining herself, she returned it to its proper place in her bathroom behind the towels.

"I don't know what came over me," she said many years later, "but I just couldn't leave Daddy's ole finger buried there. I couldn't sleep a wink knowing I'd never see it again."

Before too many years had passed she started worrying about the finger's future in our family. "Eddie Jr.," she said to me one day. "What's going to happen to Daddy's poor finger when I die? Nobody seems to love it as much as I do."

"I'll take care of it," I promised. And she replied, "That makes me feel so good. I'm going right now to put your name on it." She went into the bathroom and wrote my name on the green bottle. It was very much like writing a last will and testament.

Then a year or two later, and for what reason I never knew, she decided that she had kept Grandfather's finger long enough. The next time I was home, she left the green bottle on my mother's breakfast table. When I sat down for coffee, the finger was staring me in the face. Under the bottle there was a little note from Aunt Coleta:

"Eddie Jr., this is yours."

Aunt Coleta

AUNT COLETA loved weddings, births, and baptisms, and although she did not enjoy funerals, she attended them all and wept the loudest of anybody. Today she rarely goes anywhere, and when she does, she can hardly remember a name. She has Alzheimer's disease. Her memory comes and goes. There are days when she is fairly lucid, days when she is lost in time. A few years ago she called me "Pearl." Rather than correct her I played along, talking to her as if I were Mother. All at once, she came to herself and said, "You're not Pearl! Why did you try to make me believe you were Pearl? Who are you, anyway? Are you Eddie?"

"Yes," I answered.

"Well," she replied without a trace of irritation. "I thought you were Pearl. You look so much like your mother, I can't stand it. Every time I see you coming I think one thing: Pearl. Where is Pearl?"

"She's dead, Aunt Coleta."

"Don't tell me that?" she cried. "When did she die, hon? Why didn't somebody come get me?"

I HAVE A STRONG MENTAL PICTURE of Aunt Coleta standing in Mr. Redd's commissary. The year is about 1947. She is trying on "fit yourself" eyeglasses, one pair right after another. Each time she tests a new pair she cranes her neck. She attempts to read whatever signs Mr. Redd has posted. "I can't see a thing no more," she says, "and there's not a pair of glasses in this pile that's any count." Finally, she chooses a pair in desperation. She walks to the counter. "They make me so drunk I can't stand up straight," she admits. "But I believe they're the best of the lot."

"Coleta, you need to visit an eye doctor," Redd tells her.

"I thought that's what I just did," Aunt Coleta replies.

LIKE HER MOTHER, Aunt Coleta dwelled on tragedy, especially death by drowning. Because she had never learned to swim, she had a fear of deep water and was certain that a child was going to drown in the swimming hole unless she was there to keep control with a watchful eye. Not far from Camp Ruby there was a wide bend in Big Sandy Creek. That's where everyone swam and practiced diving from a long plank slanting precariously quite some distance over the water. We called the place Lily Hole.

Aunt Coleta would stand on the very end of the homemade diving board and scream to anybody's children to stay out of the deep water. Although her voice was high-pitched and shrill, there was also a sweetness to it as well as a vibrato gone completely out of control. "Get out of the deep water, children!" she would shout. "Come on back where it's shallow—Didn't you hear me? I said, get out of the deep water and get out right now, you know I can't swim—How do you think I'd get out there to save you if you went to drowning?—Get out of the water, I said! Are you listening to me?"

She would repeat this again and again, and if we ignored her long enough she would change her approach. In a very kind but calculated voice she would say: "Be real, real sweet boys and girls and get out of the deep water right now. Mind your Aunt Cleeter and swim on back, you're liable to make her mad if you don't."

If the sweet approach didn't work she would shake a fist at the most daring swimmers and commence shouting and screeching once again:

"There's an old alligator out there, and it's going to eat you alive if you don't come back where the water's shallow—You better mind your Aunt Cleeter and mind her right now. Think how it would make her feel if that old alligator swallowed you whole— Mind your Aunt Cleeter, I said! You don't want her to come in there after you, do you?"

No, we certainly didn't want her to jump or fall into the water. She could not swim, and all we could do was dog paddle. Saving her would have been next to impossible. And yet, there she would stand with her toes hanging over the diving board. She would sway from side to side, lose her balance and fling her arms around to regain it, but not once, thankfully, did she fall. Often, we ended our swims early for fear that Aunt Coleta would drown on our account.

MY COUSINS and I had nightmares because of Aunt Coleta, and yet, she was one of our favorite aunts. She was strict, cranky, and playful, something of an eternal child. She loved to take us fishing on the creek and cook our catch over an open fire. "No fish is too small to eat, children." That was her never-changing opinion. Sometimes she fried sun perch and baby catfish that were no longer than a minnow, and by the time they were thoroughly cooked there was hardly anything left to eat. Even still, she cautioned us to watch for bones.

Aunt Coleta (right) reminiscing with Aunt Gersey

While we ate, with our backs against a tree or our feet in the water, Aunt Coleta told us stories, not exactly ghost stories, but they were scary just the same. Often she talked about a circus cat that had gotten loose in the Big Thicket. She said the animal was orange with black spots all over it. She said it had big teeth and a long tail and at night it screamed like a woman with her head cut off. Every creature or madman Aunt Coleta described screamed the same way, like a headless woman.

She warned us against going into the woods at night. She said that the big yellow cat would skin us alive, and if it didn't something else surely would. She said that bears would drag us off to their dark, smelly dens, and piney wood rooters would throw us to the ground and stab us with their long sharp tusks. She frightened us with tales of panther, which were indeed stalking the Thicket at that time, and she was forever warning us about the gypsies. "They'll put you in a feed sack and carry you off," she said. "They'll take you far, far away, and sell you for a high, high price, and Aunt Cleeter won't never get to see you any more. How do you think that would make her feel?"

"That would make her feel real bad," we'd say and she'd answer:

"Aunt Cleeter loves the little boys and girls, but only when they're sweet."

AUNT COLETA loved children and ended up being everybody's mother. A child's death would upset her like nothing else, and she could not look at a baby's grave without weeping. I don't know exactly when she discovered the secluded grave of the Mexican baby or what she was doing in that part of the woods, but I do know that the lonely little grave caused us all to shed many tears.

The grave was decorated with the child's earthly possessions: a small teacup, a saucer, a hairbrush, a comb, and seashells. It might have been the grave of a gypsy or Indian baby, but Aunt Coleta was sure that the child was Mexican. I don't know how she knew this. We never questioned her on the child's heritage. We merely accepted what she said. It was the grave of a Mexican baby, and we visited it often.

At times Aunt Coleta's eyes became cloudy with thoughts so heavy they could almost be seen hanging in the air. Suddenly, she would say, "We better go see about that little baby. I sure hope nothing's bothered it."

Off we would go, Aunt Coleta in the lead, Sissie, Clinton, and I following close behind, and after walking about twenty minutes through the woods, we would arrive at the grave. On seeing it again, Aunt Coleta would commence crying. Huge tears would roll down her cheeks. "Poor little thing," she would weep. "Wonder why it had to die so young. It's the saddest thing in the world when a baby dies."

Naturally, my cousins and I cried right along with her. "Please don't cry, Mama," Sissie would say. "That little baby's gone to heaven."

"Please don't cry, Mama," Clinton would beg. "That little baby's gone to sleep."

We even tried to convince her that the baby's grave would grow. "Next time, it'll be a little bit bigger," we said. "Next time we won't feel so sad for it. That little baby will grow up in heaven." But nothing we could say would stop her tears. Aunt Coleta said that it was good to be able to cry anytime you wanted to.

She cried a great deal in those days, but she did not believe in wasting tears on herself. She cried for everyone else, but especially for that Mexican baby. "They left it way out here all by

Children's graves (much like the one fretted over by Aunt Coleta) at the nearby Alabama-Couchatta Reservation

itself," she often said. "Maybe they just didn't want it. Maybe it just died on them, and for some reason they couldn't take it with them—I don't know what it was, children, but it has worried me to death."

For many years that baby's grave haunted her. Because she was afraid that wild animals were going to dig up the body, we had to go check on it almost every week. "Those old armadillos and rooters better not be messing with that little baby," she said. "I sure will kill them if they do."

I don't know when Aunt Coleta stopped visiting the grave; after Camp Ruby broke up and we all moved away, I suppose. Not too many years ago, however, she thought of the Mexican baby again and wondered if anyone was watching over the grave. Sissie tried her best to find it, but like so many things in the Big Thicket, the grave of the Mexican baby is no longer there.

Aunt Coleta in Her Kitchen

ONE OF AUNT COLETA'S PASSIONS was cooking. After her eyes got bad she would often ask someone to read aloud the food section in the *Houston Chronicle*. "Doesn't that sound good," she might say. "I believe I know how to change it up a little bit." She could absorb a recipe in seconds, get to the heart of it, and turn it around into something all her own. I don't think she actually sat down and planned her meals, she just got up and cooked with whatever she had that day, and somehow, each meal seemed specially prepared. That was her way.

For lunch and supper she usually served at least two kinds of meat: venison, squirrel, frog legs, or fish, along with chicken, pork, quail, or simply a strip of beefsteak that she tenderized by beating it with the edge of a saucer. Then she would flour the pulverized meat, fry it crisp, and use the drippings in the bottom of the pan for white gravy. She merely poured off some of the grease, added a spoon or two of flour directly to the hot drippings, and stirred over a low flame for a minute or two until the mixture was smooth and slightly brown. Then she added salt, pepper, and some milk, maybe a full cup. When the gravy thickened it was ready to eat.

But Aunt Coleta didn't stop with meats and gravies. Garden vegetables were also plentiful, particularly peas:

purple hull peas, krauter peas, cream peas, and black-eyed peas, all grown on a three- or four-acre field along with corn, squash, butter beans, potatoes, watermelons, and mushmelons. Okra and tomatoes were grown in the cow lot where the soil was rich with manure, and greens were grown almost anywhere. Greens were a staple: turnip greens, mustard, and collard greens particularly. Aunt Coleta often prepared a mixture of collards and mustard seasoned with smoked bacon or simply a spoon of lard, salt, and pepper.

This was not considered an unhealthy diet back then. Of course, people worked harder, or *differently*, anyway, and therefore the diet had to go along with the way they lived. Aunt Coleta's husband, Mur, for example, was a logger. He was up at three in the morning and ready to travel quite a distance into the woods where he cut logs until he couldn't stand the heat any longer, usually by early afternoon. Then he would come home, eat a large meal, and rest awhile in order to go again the next day. Aunt Coleta kept him fed. She kept us all fed.

Other than a large garden, there was also livestock: a plow horse, a milk cow, chickens, guinea fowl, and pigs. There was always ham or bacon hanging in the smokehouse, and the icebox was filled with fresh eggs, milk, heavy cream, and butter churned at home. Aunt Coleta did a lot of her baking with milk and butter from her own cow, but when the cow was running dry she would switch to evaporated milk, which she sometimes seemed to prefer.

It's safe to say that desserts were her specialty. There was always something sweet on her table. Sometimes it was yellow squash browned in sugared water and served as a condiment with the meal. But that was an exception—all other sweets were served last and usually with hot coffee. She was especially good at making caramel cake, jelly rolls, and pies. In fact, Aunt Coleta was known for her butterscotch pie, chess pie, buttermilk pie, and rat trap cheese pie.

Since she didn't write much of anything down, it's more or less guesswork trying to arrive at one of her recipes, but with the help of Hesta Myrle Smith, along with Clinton's wife, Jeanette, and Aunt Ruby Vinson I've come fairly close to some of Aunt Coleta's finest pie-baking moments.

Butterscotch pie is my favorite. There's nothing quite like it if done correctly. Most recipes today call for brown sugar, but brown sugar will not do. "It's easier," Aunt Ruby told me, "that's why they use it, but Coleta browned her own sugar. It's better that way."

Basically, this is how I think she did it.

BUTTERSCOTCH PIE

1 cup sugar
½ cup water
1 ½ cups milk
3 eggs
¼ teaspoon vanilla
3 teaspoons flour
baked pie shell

Place the sugar in a saucepan. Add the water and cook over a very low flame until the mixture is dark brown but not burned. If it burns, you must start all over again. When the sugar syrup is brown, take the pan off the flame and allow it to cool a little. Then pour the milk into a mixing bowl. Add the eggs and vanilla. Next add the flour for thickening. If you add the flour directly to the mixture it is likely to lump up. Take a little bit of the mixture and add it to the flour. Make a paste. Then make the paste a little thinner, and finally add this thin paste to the milk, eggs, and vanilla and mix thoroughly. After that, the trick is to convince these two mixtures to combine, and it's not as easy as it may seem. One is piping hot, the other is cold. If you add the cold to the hot right away the eggs will begin cooking too fast or un-evenly, and the texture of the pie will not be smooth. Either that or the sugar syrup may instantly harden and not melt down as quickly as it should. I find it's best to allow the cold mixture to warm up a bit while the hot mixture is cooling down. To deter-mine their dispositions Aunt Coleta used her finger as a ther-mometer. She could stick a finger (usually her right index finger) into either mixture and tell if it needed to be warmer or cooler. She seemed to use this gauge for just about everything in or out of the kitchen. I'm sure she must have suffered more than a few blistered fingers, at hog killing time especially. Then it was her job to take a butcher knife and scrape the hair off the dead pig. Outdoors over a wood fire she heated water in a an iron wash pot, and when it came to a rolling boil, she put out the fire and tested the temperature of the water with a finger. Every few seconds she stuck her finger into the water and pulled it out fast. She did this over and over and when the water had cooled to the perfect tem-perature she used it to soften the hog's bristles. If the water was too hot the bristles would curl and she'd never get all the hair removed (not by the roots anyway), and if the water was too cool the hair wouldn't soften at all so she'd have to start all over again. It was quite a job to get all the hair off a hog, and she became an expert at it, but please understand that I do not recommend Aunt Coleta's finger testing method—particularly if you're gauging the temperature of melted sugar. So if you're going to try this butter-scotch recipe, you must use your own good judgment and hope for the best. At the appropriate time, temperature wise, pour the cool mixture into the sauce pan with the browned sugar syrup and stir over a low flame until you have a fairly thick pie filling. Next spoon it into a baked pie shell and let it cool. It's best when cold. Absolutely no topping is needed.

Butterscotch is an old flavor. One most people do not consider much anymore. Indeed, hardly anyone knows exactly what it is. To me it represents Aunt Coleta at her best.

Buttermilk pie is another favorite. It is both sweet and tart, very French in flavor and texture; utterly delicious. This recipe came from Aunt Coleta's 1934 cookbook, and from all the ones I've collected and tried, it comes the closest to matching my taste memory.

BUTTERMILK PIE

⅔ cup sugar
1 tablespoon flour
½ tablespoon butter
1 cup buttermilk
1 teaspoon lemon flavoring
salt
1 tablespoon lemon juice
2 egg yolks, slightly beaten
unbaked pie shell

Combine the sugar, flour, and butter. Then add the buttermilk, lemon flavoring, a pinch of salt, the lemon juice, and the egg yolks. Pour the mixture into a pie shell and bake at 425 degrees until the top browns slightly and a knife comes out clean.

Regarding buttermilk: Aunt Coleta made her own, but I'm not sure exactly how she did it. All I remember is a large glass jar with wooden blades that stirred the milk. The blades were attached to a hand crank on the lid, and Aunt Coleta tucked the jar under her arm and cranked the handle while talking to neighbors or just wandering from room to room in search of something. On busy days she might crank her way out to the cow lot to pick a few tomatoes or okra and then crank her way back home again. She could have been making butter for all I know, but whatever it was she was diligent about the process. The jar with the hand crank seemed to be permanently attached to her body like another arm or leg.

As far as her chess pie is concerned, don't ask me how she did it. It was made with corn meal, sugar, and vinegar. That's about all I know. My aunt's way with chess pie seems to be lost forever. Every attempt on my part has been a disaster, but the rat trap cheese pie is still around. Hesta Myrle makes it herself and gave me the recipe, which is accurate through and through.

RAT TRAP CHEESE PIE

1 ½ cups rat cheese
2 eggs
1 ½ cups sugar
salt
1 ½ cups evaporated milk
unbaked pie shell

Grate the rat cheese into a double boiler. Add the eggs, sugar, and a dash of salt. Then introduce the evaporated milk. Cook over a low flame, stirring constantly until the cheese melts and the mixture thickens. This may take half an hour or more, and the cheese, if it is truly rat cheese, will never fully melt. It will have a rough, almost grainy texture. Pour mixture into a pie shell and place it in a 350-degree oven just long enough for the crust to brown.

In case you don't know, rat trap cheese, commonly called "rat cheese," is the preferred cheese of all mice and rats. It is of the cheddar variety and should be purchased in wheels. It is yellow and very oily. If left unrefrigerated for any length of time, the oil comes to the surface and the color changes to that of a very ripe pumpkin. If you cannot find such a cheese, use any kind of cheddar, mild or sharp. But bear in mind: no matter what kind of cheese you use, this pie is extremely heavy and cannot be served with just anything. It is an acquired taste, for sure, and a very old one. It should be presented in a firm, flaky crust, which is not always easy to produce, especially since everyone has a different method for making it. Most people use cold water. My cousin Jeanette starts with a fourth of a cup of boiling water poured over a half a cup of shortening. After the shortening melts, she adds one and a half cups of pastry flour and a fourth of a teaspoon of salt. Then she mixes thoroughly but as little as possible. Too much handling ruins the dough.

The shortening Aunt Coleta used was lard. Truly, it makes the best pie crust ever. She mixed the lard with flour and cold water. I don't know her proportions. She just mixed until the dough felt right to her hands and that was that. Almost everything she did was by touch, and if she flopped on something, she would outright admit it. "I've done something wrong," she would say. "This may not be worth eating this time." But everything was always worth eating, even the flops. Somehow she managed to save them.

It goes without saying, Aunt Coleta was famous for her table, a round table filled with the most extraordinary variety of food. It seemed that she just cooked and cooked and kept on cooking until there was no more room on her table for another platter and then she stopped. When people dropped by to visit they were expected to sit down and eat a bite of whatever was left over or at least enjoy a cup of coffee. That was hospitality, the rule of the house. With everyone sitting around the table, Mur would say to his guests, "Back your ears and dive in."

Everyone enjoyed going to Aunt Coleta's house for a meal. And everyone still talks about her pies.

Once when I was sitting in Rapture's Heights with Hardy Cain, he told me that he would have married Aunt Coleta for her pies alone, but she wouldn't give him the eye, so he finally backed off and left her alone.

"That was a good thing," my mother said, sometime later. "For we're kin to everybody in the state of Texas. That's why I chose a soldier boy from up north. I sure didn't want to get saddled with a cousin."

"Don't tell me we're kin to Hardy Cain too," Aunt Coleta cried. "If we are, I, for one, will certainly not claim."

Rapture's Heights

HARDY CAIN once told me that my grandfather was the bravest man who ever lived. "Old Man Brown hired me when nobody else would touch a man who studied such kinds of foolishness," he said. "That takes some kind of courage."

When I came to know him, Hardy was spending most of his time in a fallout shelter called Rapture's Heights. The shelter was attached to his house but you entered it from the back porch. The door to Rapture's Heights was narrow and low, the walls were thick, and the roof was shaped like the bridge of a violin. "Rapture's Height" was written on a wall with white paint, but Hardy never referred to this place and state of mind in the singular, he always said, "Rapture's Heights." In Rapture's Heights, Christmas tinsel hung from the ceiling all year long, and on every chair and table there was a fiddle or a fiddlelike instrument, each handmade from various kinds of wood. Without being asked, Hardy would gladly play each instrument so his frequent visitors could hear the different tones. Well into the concert he would usually interrupt himself:

"I knew what every durn one of these fiddles would sound like before I made them."

He said that he could hear music in everything. When walking through the woods, he often came upon a tree

Hardy Cain, Rapture's Heights

Hardy Cain drawing the music out of a fiddle

with music trapped inside it. If the music was contained within a small section of the tree, that's the part he sawed away and carried back to Rapture's Heights, where he split the wood, carved it, sanded it, and eventually turned it into another fiddle. On completing the new instrument he would release the music he had heard by spending an afternoon playing what he called his "Old Jealous Tune." It was one of the few songs he could play all the way through. And no matter what tune he started out with, he always ended up playing the jealous tune over and over. Sometimes he called it "That Old Repetitious Tune."

"I'm going to play 'That Old Repetitious Tune' for you today," he would announce as though standing in a concert hall. "It won't let me play anything else because it's jealous of every other tune a man's got sense enough to play."

Scattered throughout Rapture's Heights were fiddles of all sizes and tones, some made of hickory, some of pine, sweet gum, holly, cedar, sycamore. "Sometimes I have to come in here and play every durn one of them before the day's out," Hardy said. "They won't give me rest until I've turned some attention on them. I can hear them begging to be played."

He believed that fiddling was the best medicine in the world to calm a man's nerves. "Let me ask you something," he said to all his visitors. "How do you think I discovered Rapture's Heights, anyway? I tell you how: I came in here and fiddled and fiddled and fiddled until I fiddled my way up there."

To Hardy, Rapture's Heights was a state of mind. It was music. It was his way of looking at the universe. And it was also a room he built for the sake of solitude. "That woman," he would say, referring to his wife, Daisy, "was about to run me out of my mind. She didn't want fiddle playing inside the house, so I had to build me a shelter to be myself in."

On one wall in Rapture's Heights hung a diagram of Hardy's universe. It was similar to an astrological chart. Daisy said it made her drunk to look at it. A green spot in the center of the diagram was surrounded by various orbiting stars and planets. There were rings of air that we breathe and rings of air that we don't breathe or can't breathe. And there were also various realms inhabited by celestial beings, all orbiting Rapture's Heights, the green spot in the center.

"That's where everybody wants to be whether they know it or not," Hardy said. "Everybody has his eye on Rapture's Heights these days, and that's why I have so durn many visitors."

Before he discovered Rapture's Heights, Hardy made a study of the stars. He built a tower called the Scaffold to the Sky, and from there he learned the heavens. No matter how much Daisy may have protested, he slept on the Scaffold to the Sky almost every night and refused to receive visitors there. "A man's got some thinking to do way up here," he said. "He can't be bothered with other people."

Somewhere between the Scaffold to the Sky and Rapture's Heights, he decided that he needed a lake on his property. When he told his neighbors he was going to dig the lake himself, they asked, "What with?" and Hardy answered, "A bucket and a shovel."

"He's crazy for sure," everyone said. "Nobody in his right mind wants a lake bad enough to dig it with a bucket and a shovel."

Nobody but Hardy. Five years later he had him a lake. His bucket and shovel were worn out, but the lake was filled with water and fish captured from a nearby creek. He said that his inspiration for digging a lake the hard way came from the earthworm. "Let me tell you something," he said. "The earthworm's the most intelligent creature in the universe. Have you ever seen anything as soft as one is that can still bore a hole through hard clay?"

Hardy not only admired the diligence of the earthworm but the beaver as well. His admiration for the beaver, however, did not last long. After he had finished his lake, a family of beavers began damming it up, and before long there were more dams than lake. Then he dragged a chair to the water's edge and serenaded the intruders with his jealous tune.

"Let me tell you how to get the beavers out of your pond without killing them," he said to anyone who would listen. "All you have to do is play some music they don't like. They didn't have the constitution it took to listen to my fiddling, so they moved to somebody else's pond."

Hardy was the Orpheus of the Big Thicket. Every day he descended into the dark underworld of Rapture's Heights, and toward evening he emerged with music. More often than not, however, it was music to his ears alone. Whereas Orpheus tamed the animals with music, Hardy ran them away.

He almost ran Daisy away also. She couldn't stand his infernal fiddling, and she didn't like his visitors any better.

Toward the end of his life, he was written up in one of the Houston newspapers, and the article attracted a wide assortment of curiosity seekers to his door. Pretty soon, Daisy was so tired of a constant stream of strangers in and out of her house that she didn't want any of Hardy's old friends visiting him either.

One day when Sissie and I decided to pay Hardy a visit, Daisy came running down the front steps to meet us. Before we were out of the car she was screaming:

"Hardy ain't home. You'll have to leave now. You can't come inside today because Hardy ain't here. I don't know where he went to, but he ain't coming back anytime soon, so you better go on about your business."

Suddenly, Hardy came running out of the house. "Don't listen to that crazy woman," he shouted. "Get out and come on in. Let's go sit in Rapture's Heights. That's what you're here for, ain't it?"

On many occasions, while sitting in Rapture's Heights and listening to Hardy play his fiddles, Daisy would sneak up behind him and whisper, "You people better go now. Hardy ain't right in the head. He don't know what he's trying to do because he ain't got much sense. I believe you'll get him started on something he don't need to be thinking about, so you better be on your way."

Now and again, she succeeded in running us off. "I can't stand no more of this racket," she would scream. "I can hear that fiddle clear inside the house."

Everyone in that corner of the Thicket said that Hardy had driven Daisy crazy with his fiddling, but Hardy said, "She was crazy to begin with. Fiddle music might run you off, but it sure won't run you crazy."

Hardy never failed to remind his visitors that fiddling was the best medicine in the world. "All a man needs is something to fiddle with," he said. "You just fiddle and fiddle and fiddle until you fiddle your way to Rapture's Heights, and when you get up there you'll know exactly where you are, even if you ain't never been there before."

"A MAN as crazy as that ought to be knocked in the head," Aunt Coleta said. "And that's why I didn't give Hardy Cain the eye."

The Davises of Double Branches

Aunt Coleta married Mur Davis, a man with eyes. They saw everything, through everything, seemed to penetrate thoughts. As a child, I was never comfortable with Mur. He seemed to know too much about me, more than I knew about myself. He knew with his eyes. If they fixed on you, you felt them like two hot coals on your skin.

He lived in a hamlet called Double Branches located between the forks of Menard Creek. It was, and still is, something of a family settlement. The old home place is still there, and many water wells are scattered about marking areas where other houses once stood. The house where Mur was raised, and where his brother Lev still lives, is a dog-run construction. An open air hallway, the dog run, divides the house through the center. Rooms are on both sides. In this case the dog run is L-shaped with three open ends, designed to separate the living quarters from the kitchen, where Mur's mother, Betty Lowe, ruled the family over a wood-burning stove.

The house sits on hardwood blocks about a foot off the ground, and the yard is still bare of grass. Hardly anyone planted grass in their yards in those days. The topsoil was gradually brushed away, and what was left was either hard clay or sand. The Davis's yard was fairly sandy, but firmly packed. Every morning Mur's mother swept the yard with a brush broom made of many dogwood branches all tied together. The broom left lines in the packed sand, and Betty Lowe seemed to have some design in mind while she brushed. The yard was serene, particularly when sitting on the porch and staring into that labyrinth of lines. But then, toward late morning, the guinea fowl would start chasing each other through the dog run and over the yard, adding their own footprints on top of the already fading lines. By midafternoon there would be little or nothing left except scratches in the sand.

Hardly any flowers were planted in the yard. Maybe a lily of some kind, but not up against the house, further away, over near the unpainted picket fence or out back by the well. Of course, there were trees, mostly sweet gum or sycamore, and if memory serves me, there was once a rose of Sharon that was allowed to get big and take over, but its place was outside the yard, somewhere in the distance where it could be seen but was no bother.

Aunt Coleta's yard was just the same. She brushed it every morning and sometimes she would brush her mother-in-law's yard as well. They had a very close and feisty relationship.

Mur's mother was a spirited lady who enjoyed dressing up in disguises and frightening all her son's wives. She would masquerade as a tramp begging food door to door, and Aunt Coleta always fell for this trick. She would prepare a plate for any beggar who knocked at her door. "How do we know it's not one of God's angels," she would say. "The Bible says we will be visited by angels when we least expect them."

But the strange visitor begging at Aunt Coleta's door was never an angel of the Lord, only her husband's mother wearing rags: a man's suit, boots, a glued-on mustache, and a brimmed hat pulled low over her face. Aunt Coleta would hand the "beggar" a plate of food, and suddenly her mother-in-law would throw off her hat and say, "Cleeter, I fooled you again, didn't I."

Then Aunt Coleta would curse a blue streak. "I hate you," she would scream, "for you have caused me to say bad words, and act ugly."

MUR'S FATHER, Poppa Davis, was a quiet, retiring man, a logger by profession, who had been born with a veil over his face, the mark of a seer. One day he saw Sister Lowe, one of his wife's relatives, walking down the lane. She disappeared before his eyes, and he didn't know what to make of it. She was there, and suddenly she wasn't. He saw Sissie that way too. She appeared to him in a dream that wasn't a dream. She walked into the room and walked out again. No words were exchanged, and no meaning was fixed to these experiences, but when he saw three white doves fly into his house and light on the mantel he knew death was imminent. He thought first of himself and his brothers, but the doves, as it turned out, had come for his grandsons: one by one three of them were killed in automobile accidents.

Although visions kept coming to him, Poppa Davis did not *see* everything. He had a brother who committed suicide, but the warning he received did not register as a warning. The brother's name was Curtis. As a young man he drank a bottle of strychnine and survived. Everyone said that it had to have been a miracle that put him on his feet again. Twenty years later, he appeared to be doing just fine, when suddenly something came over him, something that no one saw coming. After plowing the cornfield, he went home and greeted the family sitting in what was called

Uncle Mur

the Big Room. "I'm going to take me a good long rest now," he said. No one, not even Poppa Davis, understood what he meant.

Curtis went into his bedroom, as if to take a nap, and his wife and son went to the crib to feed the animals. When they left the house he fixed a string to the trigger of his rifle and laid it across the bed. Then he sat back in his chair and pulled the string.

Poppa Davis couldn't get over it. There seemed to be no end to his grief, and no way to explain why his brother had taken his life without warning, without showing a sign of anything that might have been bothering him. For the longest time Mur's father studied the cornfield, examining the rows Curtis had plowed during the last few hours of his life. They were straight rows. The straightest rows a man and a horse could plow. They were evenly spaced, no crooks, no curves, just arrow-straight rows. While plowing them he must have known what he was going to do, and he must have been at ease with his decision or else the rows would have surely turned out crooked. That was Poppa Davis's thinking.

Following the marks of the plow, he walked back and forth from one end of the cornfield to the other, searching for a clue of any kind, for a glimpse into his brother's mind, but nothing came to him, not even a vision. The vision, as it turned out, was not meant for him, it was meant for Mur.

One afternoon, while Mur was lying down, he heard the screen door slam. His uncle Curtis walked into the room and sat on the bed. "I'm going to tell you why I did it," he said, "but the only person you can tell is your daddy." Then he told Mur why he had killed himself, and straightaway Mur went to his grieving father and told him what Curtis had said. Poppa Davis listened and was immediately satisfied. His grief vanished. He understood. But no one else ever did.

No matter how much we begged, Mur refused to tell us what his brother's ghost had told him. He also made sure that no one ever forgot that he had been given a message, one that he was not allowed to speak. "I can't tell it," he would say in a calm voice. "I was told not to. When you're told something in a vision, you better mind what you're told."

Mur and his father took the message to their graves.

Many of the Davises were like that. They seemed to be in touch with the world beyond the world and the world beyond that. Mur knew things with his eyes. If they fell upon you, they ate you alive, they understood who you were and what you were all about.

His third cousin, Maynard, was of the same cut. He gave the impression that he traveled frequently between this world and the next, but unlike Mur, he did not have penetrating eyes. He did not know things without experiencing them. His knowing was firsthand. He had been there. He had seen. He remembered everything. And he never allowed any of us to forget who he was, where he had been, and that he was responsible for killing thousands of innocent people.

Maynard Davis

IN OUR small corner of the world, Maynard Davis was talked about more than anyone else. He also did more talking than anyone I have ever known. What his talking amounted to was a fifty-year monologue repeated incessantly to anyone with the patience to listen. He was something of a recluse, but when he needed company he would make door-to-door visits, and it was impossible to get rid of him or shut him up. No matter what was on his mind, be it dreadfully serious or just some wild tale that amused him, he spoke in no uncertain terms. His talk was to the point, as straight as a martin to its gourd. (Fortunately, Lynn Lennon and I recorded him at his best.)

Calling himself the most God-sent man who ever walked the earth, he began his litany with an account of his Army career. He said that he was the only man in the world who had been thrown out of boot camp as well as paradise.

During World War II Maynard was drafted. He had never been outside the Big Thicket and had no idea what kind of world awaited him. In boot camp, his feet blistered and swelled. He reported them on the sick book four times without results, and before long they were so swollen he could hardly walk, but he continued his basic training anyway. "I won't beg a man to do nothing for me," he told us countless times. "After I reported my feet for the fourth time, and nobody did a thing, I just got up and marched on them. I said, *I'll walk on you if you come off to my knees.* The next thing I knew arthritis-rheumatiz went to setting up on me, and it gave me a hot fever. And so when they got me to the hospital that old doctor, boys, he cussed everything that moved, and he told them, says: *They've kept this man out there and nearly killed him.* Says: *They've ruined him for life.* Says: *He won't never be no more count.* I didn't even know at the time what arthritis-rheumatiz were. He didn't call it rheumatiz, he just called it arthritis, and I didn't know what arthritis were. Now if he'd put the rheumatiz to it I'd of known what the old gentleman was talking about, but he didn't put the rheumatiz to it, and I just wondered to myself: *Well, I just wonder what arthritis is, anyway?* But after later-on-years I found out what it were. It went to spreading all over me—my fingers, my toes, my ears, everywhere you can name, there it was. So they put me in that *dastard institute* and

Maynard Davis

slammed me full of shots, and I ain't never been the same since."

No one was ever certain which institute Maynard was talking about. It seemed as though all the hospitals he had ever been in had merged into one larger-than-life institution where he was slammed full of shots and sent back home.

This much we know: After he was discharged from the Army he made frequent visits to the veterans hospital in Houston where he was under treatment, supposedly for diabetes. He would take the Greyhound bus there and back again. No one accompanied him. And no one ever understood the exact course of his treatment. All we know is that one day Maynard returned to the Thicket with a different look in his eye. He said that he had been wading in the wrong pond of water. And from then on he was convinced that he had committed one of the most inhumane acts of our century. He had dropped the atomic bomb.

Maynard's Story

HOLDING UP his right index finger he would say:

"I pulled the trigger with this very finger. This is the very finger I did it with. First they slammed me full of shots and knocked me out. The next thing I knew they were taking me into an airplane on a stretcher. They had me knocked out, but at times I would come to on them. I come to on them three or four different times, and when we went to drop that bomb the copilot came and got me out of my bunk. And I was like the old doctor I was telling you about, I cussed him every time he opened his mouth. Poor fellow, I ought not to of done it, but I was knocked out and didn't know half the time what I was doing. They took me around to

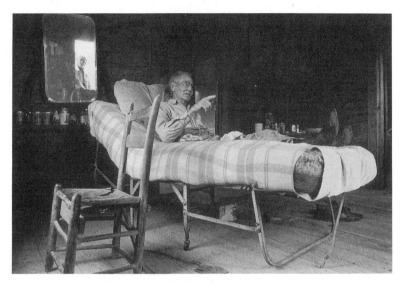

Maynard Davis relating how he dropped the atomic bomb

this room, and the copilot mashed the button on the dash, and that bomb just came cadillacking down the aisle and settled right over the hole where it went out. And then the copilot got an old piece of a ladder and leaned it up there and told me, says: *You step up on there.* Well I stepped up there and ran my finger in that pin. And then he says, *Now don't you pull until I tell you to, and when you do pull it, I mean pull. Don't you fool around about it, just jerk it as hard as you can jerk it and then get loose from it.* Well, when the time came, I just fell backwards on it. I pulled it just as hard as I could jerk it and turned it a-loose and it hit . . . I don't know what it hit, the wall of that plane or something, but whatever it was I never heard such a racket as it was making. The copilot, he said, *My God, you're going to tear the plane up.* And here's the very words I told him, I says: *Let the goddamn son of a bitch tear up if it wants to.* So he says: *My God, man, don't talk that way.* And then he says: *We've got to get this man back to bed.* And so he got me back to bed. And just about the time we got back to that bed the power of that bomb came up. Boys, if an airplane ever went to cutting up, it done everything, I guess, but roll plumb over. It was throwing us in every direction and the pilot was hollering: *Catch something and hold on to it.* And I told him, says: *There ain't a goddamn thing to catch hold of.* And he says: *My God, don't talk that way, this airplane's about to fall with us in it.* And I says: *Let the goddamn son of a bitch fall if it wants to.* I was cussing him every time he opened his mouth until that plane leveled off. And then the copilot, he said: *Oh, this man can cuss the very hardest and more of it than ever I've seen.* And the pilot told him, says: *Well leave him alone.* Says: *He don't care no way.* And so I went on and I begged them to let me look back at it. And finally the pilot said, *Carry him over to the window and let him look back and see what he's done.* But I hadn't done no more than they had done. We had done a thing we was made to do. So he carried me over to the window, and I looked back, and I know you've seen cars coming down graded roads. Maybe you was off somewhere way over yonder and you could see them when it was real dry and the dust was coming up. Well that bomb, it looked like fifty cars coming down a dirt road."

How many times were we made to listen to his story? Hundreds it seems to me. Maynard delivered it with the eloquence of a Shakespearean actor or a Greek messenger with something urgent to impart.

He had taken the sins of the world upon his shoulders, and he was prepared to die with them as well.

A year before Maynard's death, he was visiting Mur and Coleta when he started talking about the atomic bomb once again. By then Mur had heard the story so many times, he, like the rest of us, knew almost every word of it by heart. He was in the last year of his life, himself. His health was bad, and his patience had worn thin, so he silenced Maynard by telling him that he had heard the atomic bomb story for almost fifty years and he was tired of hearing it. He said that he knew that it wasn't true and didn't know why Maynard couldn't admit it. Of course, Maynard got mad. He walked out. He said he would never come back. And he didn't. He went out of his way to avoid Mur. He turned his head, averted his eyes. And the two men never spoke again.

They died of natural causes in December of 1993. They were in their early eighties. Mur was the first to go. Thirty minutes later, Maynard followed him.

We assume they are speaking in paradise.

Were Maynard alive today he might describe his December death as his second death, not his first one; the first death occurred in that *dastard institute* he was always talking about: He said that *they* killed him there. *They* strapped wires all over his head and electrocuted him. Killed him just as dead as a nit, and when he died he went straight back to *it*. And when he got there, he saw the Lord. He saw Him walk, and he saw Him talk, and he saw Him clamp both hands and shake them over his head. And he heard Him shout: *Woe be unto them people who did you this way.*

"Every word He speaks is sort of like a proverb," Maynard said. "If you study it on down, all what He speaks will give you the right thing. Sometimes you'll have to study it on down for a good long time, and then all at once His words will go to coming to you, they'll go to meaning something to you. Now, you might not always like what He's got on His mind, but you'll have to listen to it anyway. *It's* not going to hurt you, and *He's* not going to hurt you, but if something comes along that kills you He'll take your spiritualist soul with Him, and if for some reason He can't take your spiritualist soul with Him He'll send it back to your body wherever it's at."

After dying in the institute, Maynard said that his spiritualist soul was sent to paradise and kept there until the Lord figured out what to do with him. He said that paradise was spotless, and that everyone ran around with their heads shaved because hair, especially long hair, collected filth. Time and again he reminded us that there was nothing filthy in heaven, and anyone lucky enough to be accepted beyond the pearly gates would never even have to wash or change clothes, or eat a bite of food, or drink a drop of water. "In paradise, you're just a shadow," he said. "Your clothes are painted on you. Your clothes are just like paint on anything. That's His way. That's the way it is. And He won't put up with foolishness either. If when you're up there, you do something you aren't to do—why, you can't, but if you tried to—he'd chunk you out right there and then. But you can't do nothing all the way, because you're in His mind and His thoughts when you're there. You won't even have a brain. Not like the kind you have now. You'll have His brains. You'll have His spiritualist mind. You'll be in His mind, and His thoughts, all the time you're with Him."

But Maynard did not stay in paradise long. The Lord did not wish to keep him. And it was here that he usually brought his fifty-year monologue to a conclusion:

"We was all laying there side by side and the Lord came along sticking His finger in everybody's stomach, and when He got to me He told the guard, says: *I'm sending this man back to Earth*—So that's what I'm talking about when I tell you I'm *God-sent.* I was sent back to Earth as the most God-sent man that ever lived. And now I'm going to tell you all something else that you don't know. I'm doubtful any one of you knows it. I can walk by you out there where you're bunched up with somebody talking. And if any one of you says anything that's too much out of the way by me, God tells me of it. It comes right on in my mind. So you see what I'm telling you. You have to be careful coming around me and talking like you do because I'm told of it. I was a God-sent man, and they did me wrong over that bomb. They was wading in the wrong pond of water—they waded off in it, and had me wading off in it too. What they did, they frauded me, and the Lord took it that they was frauding Him too. He knew that I was in the wrong pond of water and didn't want to be there. He knew they forced me to wade out in it."

The Widow Who Lived on the Hill

I HOLD MANY MEMORIES of Camp Ruby and the surrounding communities: fishing off the bridge at Double Branches, eating hot melons in the field with my cousins, watching Aunt Coleta swaying back and forth on the diving board, and listening to Maynard Davis's ongoing litany about the atomic bomb, his family way, or some no count dog that decided to come live with him. Animals were always taking up with Maynard.

But for some reason I cannot name, my memory of Mother during that period and in those places is very dim; only on a few occasions does she stand out from the other members of the family. Later on her hour would come, but then she was very much in the background—at least for me she was.

She had a love for traveling movies, that I do remember, and in Camp Ruby a movie under a flapping tent was a special occasion. Most of the films we saw were silent. The audience sat on hard benches, and Mother read the dialogue aloud to me and anyone else sitting nearby. She was a good reader. She had a melodious voice and a natural lilt. Many people suspected her of being a singer, but she wasn't. She could hardly carry a tune and wanted to sing more than anything.

I also remember her when we sunned our beds. If the night skies were clear, the mattresses were left outdoors for another day of sunning and Mother would sleep on hers. She would lie in the dark and count the stars aloud. Falling stars thrilled her. She wished on each of them, but she never divulged her wishes. "Some things cannot be talked about," she said.

She had her secrets, and she guarded them.

MY MOTHER AND FATHER met quite by accident, or so everyone in the family has said. Mother was never convinced of it. She believed that some things were meant to be. My father, from Pennsylvania, was stationed in Bastrop, Texas, during World War II, and my mother, who was born in nearby Camden, was introduced to him by a first cousin. His name was Edward Franklin Swift; hers, Pearl Elizabeth Brown.

When they met, Mother was a telephone operator in Livingston. That was her first job, and for the rest of her life she talked about the thrill of placing long-distance calls. "Hooking people up across the country was like traveling," she said. "In those days, talking long distance was like going somewhere you'd never been before."

Because telephone operators made very little money, Mother, living in a rooming house, decided to cut her expenses even further by occasionally sharing her landlady's bed in order to make room for unexpected travelers. Mother often told me that her landlady was very fat and ignorant of personal hygiene. Throughout her life she would suddenly remember the woman.

"Honey," she would say, puffing on a Lucky Strike, "it makes my skin crawl to think about sleeping with that sorry old thing. Your father came along just in time."

Many years later, after my father was killed in combat, Mother and I were driving through Cleveland when she suddenly stopped the car in front of a hotel. "I've got to show you something," she said. We got out of the car and stood on the sidewalk.

It was a summer afternoon in the early fifties, and Mother still had that war-bride look about her. Dressed in a suit from the forties, she stood on the sidewalk and studied the front of the hotel. Then she pointed to a window on the third floor. "That's it," she said. "That's where your father and I spent our first night together. We were madly in love."

That day I heard, for the first time, an almost tangible sadness in her voice, and for the rest of her life I continued to hear it. Even when she was happy and making jokes, which was often; even when she was dancing the Charleston, which she loved passionately, she was surrounded by a sorrow she tried, sometimes successfully, to conceal. The truth is, she never fully recovered from my father's death.

"You don't get over something like that," she would say. "You just go on the best you can."

Her darkest periods of mourning, although severe, were never debilitating. She did not take to her bed and weep. She did not sit down in despair. She kept moving. She kept busy. She would get all dressed up just to go to the grocery store, and although her mood seemed lighthearted, the dark drama going on inside escaped, almost unnoticeable.

Everyone encouraged her to remarry, everyone except my grandmother, that is. She was a diabetic, terrified of being left alone, and was never as ill as she professed or as well as she might have wished. She lived under the fear that my mother would recover from my father's death, remarry, and abandon her.

"Your place is with me," Grandmother told her repeatedly. "I'm the one who really needs you."

Contrary to what Grandmother believed, Mother had no interest in remarrying, even though she had many handsome suitors.

Pearl Elizabeth Swift and Edward Swift at the army base in Bastrop, Texas, late 1942

My paternal grandmother begged Mother to marry one of the eligible bachelors in town, but Mother said that she had never met anyone quite like my father, and for that reason she chose to remain single. She called herself "the old widow on the hill." We did not live on a hill, but that made very little difference to Mother. She liked the phrase. It rolled off her tongue, and she seemed to enjoy saying it.

She would amuse herself by saying: "Get out of my way, Mr. So'n'so. I have things to do today and can't be bothered with you, for I am nothing but a tired old widow who lives on a hill, and I deserve some respect."

While chain-smoking her Luckies, a habit she picked up from my father and never dropped, she made good use of her eternal widowhood. "Don't you even so much as think of taking advantage of an old widow who lives on a hill four miles outside the Woodville city limits," she would say to anyone she thought might cheat her. There she would stand, in the face of God Himself if she had to, and in a melodious voice demand her rights.

Although her heart was often aching, and she was frequently given to bouts of self-doubt, she attempted to put a face on it all. She would flash her bright smile, her opal rings and scarlet nails, while explaining to a banker exactly why he should give the old widow who lived on the hill a small loan.

To my knowledge, no one ever refused her. Most of the men in Woodville called her Miss Pearl, and although she seemed to have nerves of steel, she was actually quite fragile inside. And yet when her confidence was high, she could give the impression that she was a tiger ready to claw her way out of any cage.

Any cage except the one she lived in, created, in part, by my grandmother's feigned dependence upon a caretaker and my mother's need to have something or, preferably, someone to occupy every minute of her time, particularly during those first few years after my father's death. Grandmother wanted constant attention, and she said that Mother was the only daughter out of three who knew how to give it. Her security was severely threatened by Mother's astounding beauty, which drew a number of bachelors to our door.

One by one they would come calling, and Mother would turn them away while Grandmother watched with small, stinging eyes. Quite frequently, with Grandmother watching from another room or listening from the porch, Mother charmed her suitors with her opals and pearls, her intoxicating smile, her laughter, and what appeared to be self-assurance.

She also charmed men by the way she smoked. Holding a cigarette between her thumb and index finger, she slowly brought it to the center of her painted lips, inhaled deeply, and exhaled through her nose. She had seen a movie star do this, probably Carole Lombard. For a long time Mother thought that Carole Lombard had hung the moon, then it was Dolores del Rio. She said that they had *presence*. They were glamorous, and interesting to watch. But then she always gravitated toward women who smoked. She didn't think smoking was unhealthy. No one did in those days. But she did think it was terribly glamorous, and on her it was. When Mother lit a cigarette, men turned to stare.

She could blow the tiniest smoke rings imaginable and enjoyed demonstrating this practiced skill in public, particularly if we were out of town. For several consecutive summers we spent a few days in Galveston, where I underwent a series of operations to remove a facial birthmark. Mother relished this time away from Grandmother. In fact, she seemed to look forward to my trips to the hospital. Since I was usually an outpatient, we were free to roam Galveston Island, I with a bandaged face, one eye completely covered, and Mother in her best threads. We explored the seaside dives or sat on benches facing the Gulf and enjoyed the breeze. Of course, she was constantly smoking.

Once when we were surrounded by dozens of little rings of smoke, she suddenly looked around and said, "Why on earth is everyone staring at me with intentions? All people want to do is stare at a widow, and the only way they know how to stare is with intentions; what's the world coming to? All people want to do is stare and stare, especially at widows; what is so interesting about a widow, anyway?"

One of our favorite Galveston pastimes was to visit a long corridor in John Sealy Hospital where a display of body parts was on permanent exhibition. There were jars and jars of arms, legs, fingers and toes, penises of all sizes, as well as breasts, eyeballs, ears, and intestines, hearts, lungs, livers, and spleens. There were fetuses floating in formaldehyde, Siamese twins connected by their heads and stomachs. There were brains and tongues and who knows what else. The place made us squirm, and we just loved it. "Honey," Mother said, "we could get us an education right here, and I don't mean maybe. Wonder how many of these people are still living? And if they are, do they ever come here to visit themselves, and if they do, what do they think about when they see what they left behind? Lord have mercy, you're old Mother would hate to see herself in a jar. We ought to bring Daddy's finger here, don't you think?"

My cousins and I were mesmerized by Mother's long, cadenced sentences with endless repetitions and questions inserted into the middle of statements. When entertaining us children she was at her best, especially when she said illogical things in such a way that almost persuaded us to believe her. "Don't swallow a water-melon seed," she told us. "If you do a watermelon vine will grow in your stomach. Vines will come out of your ears, out of your nose and out of your mouth; you'll turn into a watermelon for sure, and then we won't know what to do with you because there's not a doctor in this country that can get rid of watermelons once they take root in your stomach."

She amused us. She enchanted us. And she made us laugh, not only by what she said but by the sight of her tall, thin body moving at top speed through the house or across the yard.

"I'm all akimbo today," she would say, her threadlike arms going off in every direction. "Just look at me, I'm akimbo."

We loved the word *akimbo* almost as much as, if not more than she. For a brief time, it was her word. Using it made her laugh, made us laugh, and it was our laughter that provoked her escape into even greater animation. While watering the yard she might suddenly break into a spastic Charleston, drenching us with jets of water and sending Grandmother scurrying from the front porch, where she often sat with her crossword puzzles, dictionaries, and romance magazines.

"Look at Mama scurvy," Mother would say, pointing with the garden hose.

She had a stock of words that she enjoyed mispronouncing, but there were several that she mispronounced with a vengeance. She always said "mysteeris" instead of "mysterious," "ba'zeer" instead of "brassiere," "wistery" instead of "wisteria," and "Ba'zil" instead of "Brazil." We children made a point of engaging her in conversations that required the use of one or several of these words. It wasn't difficult because Mother was more than willing to follow our lead.

"What do you want to be when you grow up, Aunt Pearl?" her nieces and nephews asked.

"I've always wanted to be a mysteeris person," Mother replied, "and if my eyes were as pink as an albino's I would be mysteeris, too."

From time to time a door-to-door saleslady, peddling custommade foundation garments, paid us a surprise visit. "God Almighty," mother would say. "Here comes that damn ba'zeer woman. Don't leave me alone with her for one minute for all she wants to do is measure my cup size. She's the kind of woman that enjoys touching other women and can't wait to get her hands on poor me."

On many occasions I was forced to sit in the living room while Mother's ba'zeer woman discussed cup sizes and shapes, adjustable straps, and natural uplifts. Once she turned to me and said, "Eddie, wouldn't you like to go outside and play?"

"My mother doesn't want me to," I replied. After the saleswoman left, I was severely reprimanded for saying this. "All you need to say," Mother told me, "is that you do not enjoy playing outside all by yourself. You do not need to give this woman the impression that I'm scared to be in the same room with her."

"If you'd let her take your measurements just once," Grandmother said, "she'll never have to do it again."

"I am nothing but a contrary old widow," Mother replied, "I don't have money to waste on fancy ba'zeers, nor do I have reason to wear one."

"Don't you understand," she once said to the traveling saleslady, "I don't have a bust, and I don't want one, so why do I need to invest in one of your products? I am a poor war widow with a small pension. All I have is two little hickory nuts, a sick mother, and a growing boy. I don't have a job. I can barely put food on our table, and all you want to do is talk me into buying one of your damn ba'zeers."

Mother made it sound as if we were starving to death when we really weren't. We owned our house, had very few debts, and even though both Grandmother and Mother received pensions, Mother had a lot of people convinced that we were destitute.

"Oh, I'm so hungry," she would say. "I'm so very hungry for something good, and I don't know what it is, and even if I could think of it it wouldn't do me any good because I wouldn't be able to afford it."

Once she took a job at a window factory, and before long she had her boss convinced that she could only afford one piece of steak. "I gave it to my mother," she said with a long, sad face. "I cooked it just the way she likes it. Then I put it on the table and sat down across from her, and I watched her eat every bite. She sure did enjoy it, and it smelled so good until my mouth just watered. I wanted a bite of it so bad I didn't know what to do, but I let her have it all."

Mother's boss was about to go out and buy her a big steak, but Sissie stopped him. "Pearl's got all the steak she needs," Sissie said. "She was just fooling with you. She does us all that way, sometimes."

That was only one of the little dramas Mother played over and over for her own amusement. The truth is: she loved an audience, but not a large one. Crowds made her nervous. Most of all she enjoyed making people laugh. She had a natural sense of comic delivery, and performing was certainly in her blood. Had she been born in another time or place, she might have taken to the stage. I cannot help wondering what she would have been like had my father lived. Would that have made a difference?

As it was, they had lived together only a few months. When he was killed their honeymoon was still going strong, and for the rest of her life she carried only the finest memories of him.

One day when she was going on and on about how wonderful he was, I said to her, "No one can be all that great. If you had lived together a little longer you would have seen another side of him."

"Oh no, hon," she said. "That's not it. There's much more to it than that, so much more I can't explain it right now, so I won't even try."

In her heart she was convinced that my father and she had been made for each other, that their marriage had been fixed in the stars. She did not relinquish this belief. She held on to it her entire life.

Because my father had predicted his death, Mother believed that he had the gift of prophesy. He was a master sergeant. I was eighteen months old when he died in Burma. When he said good-bye to my mother for the last time, he told her he would not return. He had a premonition of death. He just knew. I don't know how Mother reacted at the time, but many years later she said, "Some people know these things in advance. They've been touched by something nobody really understands."

At the time of my father's death we had not yet moved to Woodville. We were still living in Camp Ruby, and my grand-father was still supervising a team of loggers. He was employed by a large sawmill concern located in the nearby town of Camden where Mother spent the first seven or eight years of her life. The thing she remembered most about Camden was a community of albino Negroes. Those white black men were engraved into her memory, and she talked about them all her life.

Because I had never heard anyone else mention them, I assumed that Mother had created this community of albinos out of sheer imagination, just to give herself something else to talk about. Only recently did I found out that she had not. Hesta Myrle Smith remembers the albinos well. She said they lived in a settlement called Lily Island on the outskirts of Camden. "Not all of them were loggers. Some taught school. A few were redheaded, and all of them had pinkish-colored eyes that danced about continuously."

Hesta Myrle doesn't know where they came from or what happened to them, but Mother always said that they came from Ba'zil. She said that their eyes were pink and mysteeris, and that you could not tell if they were looking at you or not. She said that white people had severely mistreated them, and therefore they had quick tempers and were prone to carrying knives and clubs. She also said that they sunburned easily and seemed to know things ordinary people did not know. She said that my father was just the same. "The biggest difference," she said, "was complexion. He was a little darker than they."

My Mother and Her Beloved Half Sisters

RANDFATHER BROWN was twice married. With his second wife, my grandmother, he had three daughters and two sons, but with his first wife, who died young, he had two daughters, Bessie and Myrlie, both not much younger than Grandmother. Mother called them "my halfs." She and her half sisters argued constantly about everything and nothing, and yet, I don't think they ever came to a falling out.

The two half sisters were entirely different in personality and physical appearance. Aunt Bessie, now in her 90s, is small, energetic, and very thin. She is serious, fiercely opinionated, and has no time for nonsense. If she has a fault it is simply this: she has never been known to lose an argument. For as long as I can remember, Aunt Bessie's hair has been cut short and curled close to her head. She is not one to fuss over her appearance, but Aunt Myrlie, who died some years ago, was flamboyant in every way.

Aunt Myrlie was tall and had high, Indian cheekbones, a dark complexion, and long, black hair that she oiled with Vaseline before pulling it through and wrapping it around what was then called a rat. Aunt Myrlie's rat was ancient. As far as I could tell, it was a mass of artificial hair, wool, and God knows what else, shaped like a large doughnut. She used it to create a perfect bun at the nape of her neck. I don't recall her ever changing hair styles or replacing that tired, worn-out rat.

Aunt Myrlie was quite a dresser, and her face was always brightly painted. Even when she had no social obligations, she fixed her hair and face, wore stockings, fine dresses, and costume jewelry. She used perfume at home, whether expecting company or not, and she gave the visual impression that she had many very important engagements.

"You belong on Crockett Street," Mother enjoyed telling her glamorous half sister.

At that time, Beaumont's Crockett Street was known for its houses of ill repute. Once, Aunt Myrlie, with a group of her Port Arthur friends, ventured into that notorious part of town to eat Mexican food at a popular restaurant. Mother was invited to go along, and she refused, but not without making an issue of it:

"Mexican food is not the only reason why you enjoy Crockett Street, Myrlie. Everybody knows that."

From then on Aunt Myrlie took up the issue herself. When Mother was in a foul mood, my aunt would say:

"Pearl, you need to come to Beaumont and eat some Mexican food. One hot tamale will do you the world of good."

BOTH HALF SISTERS were married. Uncle Elsie, Aunt Bessie's husband, was very calm. He spoke slowly, in a high pitched voice, and could build anything. But Uncle John, Aunt Myrlie's husband, was just the opposite. He was a nervous, white-haired man, much smaller than his wife and equally mindful of his appearance. He was always starched and ironed; even in the heat of summer there was rarely a wrinkle on him, and like Aunt Coleta and Mother, he was much loved by the children.

Uncle John had the endearing habit of announcing his actions in advance. "Eddie boy," he would say, "I believe I'm going to wave at the next truck that comes along." Soon he would go running toward the highway and wave at a diesel truck as if well acquainted with the driver. If the driver blew his horn, Uncle John would squeal with delight. He would jump around, wave with both hands, or dance a little jig.

"Why," Aunt Myrlie once asked my mother, "does John want to act like a pure fool?"

"Maybe that's just the way he is," Mother innocently replied.

If we happened to be taking a walk in the woods or even around the yard, Uncle John usually announced his next big move. "Eddie boy," he said to me one day, "I believe I'm going to make me a path right through these bushes." He bent over and plowed through the underbrush. Flinging his arms around like blades on an electric fan, he bushwhacked his way through the woods. Aunt Myrlie frequently accused my cousins and me of encouraging her husband to return to childhood.

THE HALF SISTERS lived in Port Arthur, about seventy-five miles from Woodville. On weekends they visited us with or without their husbands, and when Grandfather was dying, they came almost every weekend to help Mother care for him. He lingered in a semiconscious state for quite a long time, so the half sisters were in our house a great deal in 1951 and '52.

Mother took the greatest pleasure in making fun of her halfs, especially the flamboyant Myrlie. There was nothing they wouldn't say to each other, and often they enacted the same scenes over and over. They particularly enjoyed arguing about medical doctors and a woman's need for physical examinations.

Mother accused her painted half sister of running to every two-bit physician in the state of Texas not because she was sick but because she needed the attention. "You enjoy being examined better than any woman I've ever seen," Mother would say. "You're worse than that trash Frank brings home. All you do is run from one doctor to the next, and I know why too."

Aunt Myrlie would react as if deeply angered, but she rarely was. "Pearl," she would shout, "You need to be examined by a reliable doctor who knows his business. If that doesn't make you feel better, it will at least ease your mind to find out just what's wrong with you."

"My mind is completely at ease, thank you," Mother would reply in a sanctimonious tone. "I'm not the kind of person who enjoys showing her behind every time she turns around. I'm not like you, Myrlie."

Aunt Bessie's sharp voice would interrupt them, "Oh don't be like that. Just try to get along." She never trusted the direction these contrived spats might lead and expected one or both sisters to become very angry.

Aunt Bessie rarely entered into these doctor dialogues, but she could become very annoyed over Mother's method of introduction. She enjoyed taking her half sisters around town and introducing them as if they were debutantes on the way to a ball. "Oh, Miz So'n'so," she would say. "I'm so glad to see you. Now you can meet my *half* sisters."

"Pearl," Aunt Bessie would exclaim with resentment. "Why can't you just call us your sisters? Why do you always introduce us as your *half* sisters?"

"Because you ARE my half sisters," Mother would reply.

They carried this dialogue to great lengths and never seemed to tire of it, but they exhausted everyone else with their endless variations. And if not locking horns over the half sister issue, their conflicts seemed to have something to do with the way mother ran the house. Aunt Bessie considered herself a model homemaker. She was constantly fussing at Mother for spending too much money at the grocery store and for cleaning the inside of our house with a garden hose.

Twice a year, sometimes more often, Mother dragged the furniture into the yard. She took all the pictures off the walls and hosed down the inside of our frame house. She said it was the only way to clean your floors and get rid of all the spiders and stinging lizards. She practically flooded Grandfather's sickroom while he was lingering in bed and staring into paradise.

"You're going to rot the house to the ground," Aunt Bessie said.

"Well if I do," Mother replied, "it will at least be clean."

Greatly irritated, Aunt Bessie tried reasoning with Mother. "Pearl," she said in a pinched voice, "if you keep this up, Papa won't have a house to die in."

"Well now," Mother told her, "that's something for you to talk about isn't it?"

Nothing Aunt Bessie could say would change Mother's mind. She preferred the garden hose over the vacuum cleaner, and that was that.

During the heat of summer, she also used the garden hose to cool down the house. She drenched the window screens, the roof, and the outside walls. Sometimes she even dipped the curtains in a bucket of water and hung them back up dripping wet. Then she turned on the attic fan, and in no time the house was cool and damp. Grandmother didn't seem to mind this method of house cleaning and cooling. As long as she had something to read and a few pieces of candy hidden in her purse or brassiere she was content, but the half sisters said that Mother had lost her mind.

Mother and her halfs were constantly bickering back and forth. I would usually sit at the kitchen table and listen to them. It was, by far, the greatest show. Once they started their butcher knife routine it could last for an entire weekend. It would usually begin with one of the half sisters asking:

"Who put the butcher knife in the dishwater? I almost sliced my fingers off just now."

The other half would say, "Pearl did it. I saw her. She wants you to mutilate yourself because you're nothing but a half sister. Neither of us is good enough for her."

Then Mother would reply, "That's right. I don't know why you come here anyway." Hearing this the half sisters would swear they would never return.

Quite often, this little scene ended with Aunt Myrlie saying, "Pearl, I'm going to send you to my doctor for a complete head to toe examination, we need to find out what's wrong with you once and for all."

"Oh nothing's wrong with her," Aunt Bessie would add. "She's just been a widow too long."

"Well then," Aunt Myrlie would reply, "A *physical* is exactly what she needs."

And my mother, almost angry at this point, would shout:

"I cannot stomach the thought of it! If there's one thing I don't need it's a nasty-minded doctor putting his hands in places where they don't belong."

The Apricot Seed

MY GRANDMOTHER, Anna Elizabeth Gay, had no more love for medical doctors than my mother did. Doctors were always telling Grandmother what to eat, and that annoyed her. She had her own ideas about food and didn't want to be interfered with. She knew what she liked; she ate accordingly and was almost always sick or on verge of becoming sick—physically sick, sick at heart, or both.

It seemed that she just loved to suffer, even at the dinner table, where she would set her mouth on fire with peppers of all kinds. We had pots of bright-colored peppers growing inside the house and on both porches as well as the garden, but the plants never amounted to anything because Grandmother would not leave them alone. She had a preference for bird-eye peppers because they were the hottest, and she often ate them straight off the bushes, crushing them with what few teeth she had left. Pretty soon her face would turn bright red, and her eyes would water. "God Almighty!" she would shout, "I believe that's what you call *hot*," but she just kept on eating them anyway.

She ate everything she pleased, as a matter of fact, and that was part of her problem. She was a diabetic. She never maintained a proper diet and was always certain that she was about to die. "I believe the Good Lord will take me tonight," she frequently said. "I believe my time has come." On other occasions she changed her tone, "I believe He's going to make me suffer a long one. He made Horty suffer, I don't see why I should be any different."

She was always dreaming up the worst possible calamities and not only for herself: she included the entire family in her dark visions. Some of her cousins said that she was born that way, that it was just part of her nature, but others weren't so sure. One thing is certain, she spent her entire life dwelling on tragic occurrences: death by strangulation, by gunshot, by rape and snakebite. Death by unidentified falling objects or death under the wheels of a car, a train, or a log truck was to her as likely as a cat stealing a baby's breath away. Death by falling into a well was also a major preoccupation, as was death by falling into a vat of boiling oil. One of her uncles had died by falling into a vat of oil at the refinery in Texas City, and she never forgot it, or allowed her children or grandchildren to forget it either. Grandmother was afraid of everything that moved. She was always talking about landslides, earthquakes, or anything that might come crashing down without warning.

Children playing under the house made her particularly nervous, especially in Camp Ruby. There she lived in fear that a sudden wind would blow the houses off their blocks and that all the children playing underneath them would be smashed along with the chickens. If she spotted a storm cloud she would get down on all fours and scream to anybody's children under anybody's house: "Come out from under there right now, if this old house falls down we won't be able to tell chickens from children."

I don't think there was a time when the anticipation of tragedy or sickness of some kind did not influence Grandmother's enjoyment of life. She seemed to thrive on maintaining her dark point of view. In spite of being a diabetic, she often succumbed to her cravings for candy, sweet wine, and pastry. Her feet were forever spotted with diabetic sores, and yet she continued eating whatever she pleased, and whatever she ate usually made her quite ill. Everything, it seemed, made her ill, even car rides taken at a leisurely pace.

On Sunday afternoons Mother would drive us around Woodville to look at the yards and see what was blooming. Then she would head into the surrounding countryside. Grandmother looked forward to these outings until we were on the open highway, and then she would become nervous and fitful. She was constantly on the lookout for anything suspicious, particularly a paper bag or a cardboard box lying in the middle of the road. "Pearl," she would say, "there might be a baby in that brown paper bag, don't run over it whatever you do. We'll have to go to jail if you kill somebody's baby."

For many years my mother drove with extreme caution when Grandmother was in the car. She steered clear of anything that might arouse Grandmother's anxiety. And then one day, Mother reached a point of no return. She had had enough. From then on she ran over everything in her path. Boxes, bags, baskets, tin cans, whatever was in the road, she steered straight toward it, and with a wicked smile that made Grandmother quite angry. "You're determined to aggravate me to death, aren't you?" she would scream. "Why did you run over that box? You could have killed somebody's child."

"Oh my goodness," Mother would say in a sweet voice. "I didn't know that. Why didn't you give me some warning?"

"I've been warning you about these things all your life," Grandmother would reply. "And what good has it done?"

She enjoyed growling and complaining to everyone about Mother's reckless driving. "I'll never get in the car with her again," she would announce. "All she wants to do is kill somebody. I believe Pearl has killing on the brain. That can't be a healthy way to live."

No matter how many times she swore she would never get into Mother's car again, the moment she heard the engine start, she climbed into the passenger seat and directed my mother's every turn. Many times she threatened to jump out of the moving car if Mother didn't reform her ways. But my mother never reformed, and my grandmother never jumped. That was their unspoken understanding.

Grandmother spent her entire life with tragedy on her mind. And yet with the exception of the uncle who was boiled in oil and her younger sister, Hortense, who met an unusual and untimely death, Grandmother's life seems to have been relatively free of disaster. It was the death of beloved Horty that brought Grandmother the most grief. She had photographs of Great-Aunt Horty in her coffin. She kept them in a trunk in her bedroom, and from time to time she would sit with them on her lap and weep.

Grandmother had two sisters. Ettie, the elder, was considered the family intellectual and Hortense, the beauty. My grandmother, the middle child, thought she was worthless because she was not as pretty as Horty or as smart as Ettie, but the truth be known, Grandmother possessed the best mind of anyone in the family. She spoke in complete sentences and paragraphs, worked crossword puzzles in record time, and was a voracious reader. She was constantly adding new words to her vocabulary by reading dictionaries and encyclopedias along with the Bible, Dickens, Trollope, Brett Harte, Shakespeare, newspapers and more newspapers, romance magazines, suspense novels, and detective stories. She followed all the local and national crimes with passion and was something of an armchair criminologist. "The criminal mind intrigues her," my mother said, "to an unhealthy extent."

Grandmother and her two sisters grew up in a boardinghouse called the Gay Hotel. It was located in Cleveland, Texas. Their father, Joseph Newton Gay (a descendant of John Gay, who wrote *The Beggar's Opera*), was a well-known East Texas atheist. Their mother, Coleta Gay, was a fine businesswoman who ran the Gay Hotel until she was about eighty-five years old.

I am not sure how or what Horty and Ettie contributed to the family business, but Grandmother was known as the bed maker. Great-Grandmother Gay often said: "When Bessie smoothes a sheet it feels just like it's been ironed."

Of the three sisters, Horty was undoubtedly the favorite. She had an agreeable disposition, and from what I can gather, everyone worshipped her astounding beauty. From time to time Grandmother would force us grandchildren to gaze upon photographs of Horty surrounded by funeral wreaths. "Wasn't she beautiful?" Grandmother would say. We always dreaded this moment, because Great-Aunt Horty was far from beautiful, particularly in her coffin, and she did not appear to be as young as we had first imagined. In a demanding voice, Grandmother would repeat herself, "I said, wasn't she beautiful?"

Knowing that we would be forced to agree with her, we would stare at the floor while she repeated her question again. "Oh, yes," one of us would finally reply, "Great-Aunt Horty was just *beautiful.*" Then Grandmother would be satisfied for a while, but in another week or so, the photographs of Great-Aunt Horty would be on her lap again, and she would capture one or several of us grandchildren and force us to exclaim over our great-aunt's fine skin and lovely hair. "If you had only known her," Grandmother would weep. "She was not just beautiful on the outside, she was beautiful inside as well."

Today almost everyone in the family will agree: it was the nature of Horty's death that caused Grandmother's mind to take a sharp and very dark turn. Great-Aunt Horty died by swallowing an apricot pit. Grandmother called it a seed. It lodged crosswise in Horty's throat and over a period of two days she slowly suffocated. Grandmother said that it was a terrible death, a death no one as sweet as Horty should be made to suffer.

For as long as I can remember we were never allowed to have apricots in our house. Never. The mere mention of an apricot would send Grandmother into a weeping frenzy. She lived with an inordinate fear that her children and grandchildren would choke to death at the dinner table. She was certain that Horty's tragedy would be repeated, and she frequently warned us against fish bones, small rocks hidden in bags of beans, and bits of glass that might turn up in the bottom of a Coke bottle. Every time she saw us with a Coca-Cola she would say, "Come here and let me look in that bottle. There might be a chokeable inside it somewhere." She would snatch the bottle out of our hands and hold it up to the light. Sometimes she would even pour the drink through a tea strainer and give it back to us in a cup. Once she read an account of someone who found a tiny frog in the bottom of a bottled drink. She dwelled on this for many years and was sure it could happen anywhere, anytime.

My cousin Sissie and I did nothing to alleviate Grandmother's phobia. If anything, we contributed to it. Often we slipped off to Mr. Redd's commissary to buy toy horns, two for a nickel. Grandmother hated those horns. When she heard us blowing them she took an instant craving for candy and snuff, anything to soothe her nerves. It wasn't the noise she found so upsetting but the careless way the horns had been constructed. She was suspicious of the tiny metal whistle in the mouthpiece and was sure we would suck one of these sharp-edged devices down our throats. Sissie often explained to her that we did not suck on the horns to make the noise: we blew on them.

"But one day you're liable to forget which way to go," Grandmother would say, reaching into her bun for a hairpin. "One day you might think you're blowing when you're really sucking, and before you know it you'll suck that noisemaker down your windpipe." Then she would snatch the horns away from us, and with her hairpin she would rip out the dangerous noisemaker and give us back our silent but very safe toys. I have no idea how many nickels we spent on toy horns, only to have Grandmother mutilate them with a hairpin.

Nothing, it seemed, could ease her mind. She lived in terror of swallowing any kind of foreign object, anything slippery, sharp, or thorny that might turn up quite unexpectedly in our food. She examined every morsel with her fingers before allowing us to eat. She carefully picked the flesh off fish and mashed it between her fingers before putting it on our plates. And no matter how much she examined our food she still worried about chokeables she might have overlooked. She was particularly suspicious of mashed potatoes, thick stews, soups, and gravies, and used her fingers to search for the hidden killers: rocks, glass, seeds, hairpins, thumbtacks, bones. She would reel off the list of killers with a strange combination of horror and pleasure.

It always pleased her to find a chokeable. She would hold the object in front of our faces and say, "Had I not found this, you might have choked to death like Horty."

"Poor, poor, Aunt Horty," one of us grandchildren would reply. "She was *so* beautiful. It's such a shame she had to choke to death."

Grandmother would then accuse us of mocking her. And while she scolded us for being disrespectful, we would dive into our mashed-up food before she decided to examine it once again.

Baptism in the Big Thicket

ALTHOUGH I've never had much patience for Bible-thumping evangelists, I must admit there was one, Louise Owens, with whom I spent a great deal of time. After she learned that my grandmother had never been baptized, she visited us often and was bent on leading Grandmother to salvation, or else.

Louise lived in Woodville. She wrote plays, composed gospel songs, spoke in the unknown tongue, and when I first met her was teaching Sunday school to a class of octogenarians. She had the elderly out of their beds and wheelchairs; they were beating on tambourines, singing, dancing, clapping their hands, and telling everybody they would never die. When the deacons of the Baptist church saw the elderly behaving as if in a state of rapture, they had Louise replaced with a less spirited teacher. "I was fired," she said, "because the old people were enjoying themselves more than anybody else."

Later on, she organized her own charismatic church and became known as "Sister" Louise.

Louise was a corpulent woman with golden red hair, a color she achieved by mixing several commercial hair dyes. She had a propensity for silver lamé boots, hats and head scarves, costume jewelry, and loud colors. "God told me to wear all these colors so people will know how happy He's made me," she would say. "*Ishee-ma-Ha-ya-ma-HA*, Lord Jesus."

After the Pentecostal spirit descended upon her she was practically unstrung with happiness. On the spur of the moment she would break into peals of laughter followed by a pouring forth of the unknown tongue. No matter where she might be, she would throw back her head and shout the special language God had given her. "Louise," I once asked, "just what does *Ma-Ha-ya-ma-HA*, mean anyway?" Rolling her eyes toward heaven, she answered. "It means, *He* loves me and *I* love you." After she said this she slapped me on my forehead and shouted jubilantly, "I SEAL you in the name of Jesus." This is what she called, "placing the *seal* of Jesus on the sinners of the world." The larger the sin, the harder the slap. That seemed to be her rule.

I don't know how Louise Owens found out that my grandmother had never been baptized, but this piece of information excited her like none other. Proselytizing fires burned in her eyes and heart. You could almost see the sparks. Intent on leading my grandmother to salvation, Louise visited us several times a week. When Mother saw her coming she would run out to meet her. "Please don't seal Mama in the name of Jesus," she would beg. "She's old. You might break her neck."

Louise always promised not to slap the Holy Spirit on Grandmother's forehead, and I must say, she was a woman of her word, but that did not stop her from witnessing to my grandmother in other mysterious ways. "Miz Brown," she often said, "God has given me a new song to sing to you this afternoon. This song will surely touch your heart and save your soul." While Grandmother sat like a stone, Louise would commence singing a special God-given composition. She sang everywhere she went, the post

office, the grocery store, on every street corner, and to my Grandmother's disgust, in our living room and front yard as well. Several of her favorite songs became hits on the gospel circuit. The
most famous was:

> Oh, the Holy Ghost will set your feet a-dancing.
> The Holy Ghost will bless you through and through.
> The Holy Ghost will set your feet a-dancing,
> And set your heart a-dancing too.

There are about twelve verses to this spirited song, and Louise
sang all of them while dancing around like a blazing comet in
front of my grandmother, who sat upright, motionless, with a
grim expression on her face. Louise always tried to get my grandmother to dance and sing with her, and for this, among other
things, Grandmother hated Louise Owens.

One afternoon she arrived at our house not with a song in her
heart but with a bucket of water in her hand. She said that the
water had been blessed by a preacher she had recently uncovered,
a man touched by the Spirit of God. She called him the most
divinely inspired evangelist in the world, and with a glowing face
and glistening eyes she added: "He can preach on any subject,
anytime and anywhere."

"Yes," Grandmother replied. "And we can guess who he's been
preaching *on* too."

We never found out how the man had blessed the bucket of
water, but Louise was certain that one drop of it would save
Grandmother's soul from hell's fire and damnation. "I'm going to
baptize you, Miz Brown," she said happily. "God doesn't care anymore if you're baptized by sprinkling or total immersion. We're
now living in a new age. I'm going to drip some of this holy water

Sister Louise Owens

on your head, and then you won't have to worry about your soul anymore."

Almost out of control, Grandmother cursed Louise without mercy, and Louise fled as if the Devil were chasing her. Shortly thereafter, she disappeared, seemingly overnight. It was the first of many sudden disappearances. When questioned, members of her family didn't seem to know where she was, and if they did they weren't saying, but before long we heard that she had been sent to an insane asylum, where she was happily sharing her God-given gift for song with the lunatics.

"That suits me just fine," Grandmother said vehemently.

Outside the family Grandmother was known for modesty of speech, but inside the family she was known to swear like a sailor, if she needed to, as Louise found out for herself. Grandmother believed it was necessary to have a few curse words in her vocabulary in order to vent anger before it swept her beyond control. It was astonishing to hear a stream of profanity spewing from her thin lips. In spite of her precarious health, her dark point of view, and her reliance on invective, she was a most dignified woman who enjoyed a good laugh, as long as it wasn't at her own expense. She was crazy for butterfly sleeves, anything cut on the bias, bath powder, and sweets, especially blackberry wine.

Riddled with contradictions, she could be cursing one minute and demure and bashful the next. She was terribly sensitive about her appearance and rarely allowed her picture to be taken because of her long humpback nose and her large, pendulous breasts. Because of her breasts, she was deeply opposed to baptism by total immersion. She believed that it was vulgar for women with large breasts to be taken under the waters of everlasting life and brought back up again in front of God and everybody else with wet clothing clinging to their womanly forms. "My breasts are too big for baptism," she frequently admitted, but not without a blush. She was convinced that the only time most men went to church was when they knew that certain full-figured women were going to be baptized. "I know who I am, and what I am, and what I believe, and what I don't believe," she preached. "And that's good enough for me. Therefore, it has to be good enough for God too."

Sissie took our grandmother seriously on every account when it came to baptism. She attended Sunflower Baptist Church, a small frame building located near Big Sandy Creek. The church did not have an indoor baptismal pool, so all the Sunflower converts were baptized in Lily Hole. Sissie was about fifteen or sixteen when she was baptized, and for that unforgettable experience she chose, in spite of her skinny frame, to overdress. Taking Grandmother's advice, my cousin wore a bathing suit, several crinoline petticoats, a dress, a blouse or two, and a full skirt.

With the congregation standing on the banks of the creek, Sissie entered the waters of everlasting life and was almost swept away under the weight of so much wet clothing. Her voluminous skirt trapped air like a balloon obscuring all but the top of her head, which was wrapped in a colorful scarf. She took a few minutes to slap the air out of her baptismal costume, and then, crossing her arms over her bosom, she surrendered herself to the somewhat startled preacher. "I baptize you, my little sister," he said nervously, "in the name of the Father, and the Son, and the Holy Ghost." All at once he tilted my cousin back and gave her a fast but thorough dunking, and for a moment all that could be seen was Sissie's clothing floating on the surface of the water. Then the preacher tried to bring her to her feet again, but that was no easy matter. Her layers and layers of wet clothing were extremely heavy. She could hardly stand under the weight and required many helping hands when wading out of the creek.

Years later she said to me: "Eddie Jr., I believe I nearly drowned that day. Grandmother's wrong. Nobody needs to wear that much clothing to be baptized in."

"Well, at least she was baptized," said Eva Gay. If Grandmother thought she had a problem with Louise and the water bucket, little did she know what kind of soul-saving baptism her youngest daughter was scheming.

Eva has always been a devout believer, unswerving in her particular doctrine. Shortly after her marriage, she left the Baptist Church for the Church of Christ because she enjoyed taking the Lord's Supper every Sunday instead of once a quarter as is the custom with the Baptists. She said that taking the Lord's blood every Sunday made her feel real pure, and we were all very happy for her just as long as she did not try to drag the rest of us down her path. She was, and we assume still is, an avid believer in baptism as the only means to salvation, and she worried herself sick because her mother had never been baptized. The older Grandmother got, the more Eva Gay worried and preached and harped on the necessity of baptism, but only by immersion. "Sprinkling will not do!" she testified loudly. "You must be taken completely under the waters of salvation in order for the baptism to take." To Eva Gay baptism has always been a kind of vaccination against the wiles of the Devil.

Because she was frantic with worry over the state of her mother's soul, she proposed a solution: "Mama," she said, "what we're going to do is call the family doctor, and *my* preacher at the same time, and while they're on their way over here I'm going to fill up your bathtub with warm water. Then we're going to baptize you right here in the privacy of your own bathroom, and a few days later we'll announce your salvation in the newspapers. That way you can accept Jesus publicly, Mama."

Over a period of several days, and with carefully chosen words, Grandmother expelled her anger to keep from striking her daughter. But Eva Gay did not give up. For many years she begged her mother to accept Christ publicly and to follow Him into baptism. She prayed and pleaded, but to no avail, for Grandmother refused to enter the water.

"It's all my fault that Mama died unbaptized," Eva Gay has been known to say. "I didn't provide the right kind of example for her to follow."

But being unbaptized never seemed to bother my grandmother. Unlike her father, who professed to be an atheist and was written up in the Houston newspapers for repenting on his deathbed, Grandmother died without receiving so little as one drop of Holy water. Twenty years after her husband, Grandmother's hour arrived, and although she wasn't exactly thrilled over the experience of dying, she passed on without uttering a word of repentance or regret. She seemed secure with the state of her soul.

Grandfather on His Deathbed

I N WOODVILLE we lived in two locations but in the same house. The first location was two miles north of town. Our board-and-batten house was about fifty yards from a fire tower and a few steps more to the offices of the Texas Forest Service, where Mother worked as a secretary. During that time, Grandmother continued answering the switchboard, and Grandfather, completely disabled by then, spent most of his waking hours lying in bed. His bedroom had six large windows and was located in the back part of the house. There he sang, drank his cough remedy, and entertained visitors, old angels whom he seemed to know intimately, along with friends and enemies, long since dead, who came back to argue or sing with him. On good days, he stared at the ceiling or out the windows and shouted to my mother, "Ain't that pretty. Ain't that pretty. Daughter, come see where I'm going."

"Oh, it's just beautiful up there, Daddy," Mother said to comfort him. "I sure wish I could go with you." She said this with serious expression as if she meant every word, and I often wondered if she did.

On days when he was particularly disoriented, Grandfather tended to wander around. Lacking the ability to distinguish between indoors and outdoors, he would turn up almost anywhere. Finding the bathroom gave him the most trouble. He could never quite remember where it was. Once he peed on the Christmas tree, another time on all the presents, and finally he discovered the side porch. Day or night he would stand there singing and relieving himself at the same time. No one seemed to care what he did, or when he did it, except the men who worked at the Texas Forest Service. They told Mother that she needed to keep her father indoors where he belonged.

Of course, Mother flew in their faces with indignation. "Show some respect," she demanded. "He's an old man. He's worked hard all his life. And he's losing his mind."

We lived in the shadow of the fire tower for about a year before we were asked to move. The Texas Forest Service couldn't wait to get rid of us and made it as easy as possible for us to resettle. We had no place to go, and no house of our own, so the Forest Service just gave us the house we were living in, but under one provision: it had to be moved to another location.

Because we had no money to buy property, Grandmother called on her old friend, W. T. Carter, for help. Mr. Carter was a wealthy landowner. He also ran the large sawmill in Camden, and Grandfather had been one of his best workers. "We've got a house, but no place to put it," Grandmother told Mr. Carter. He answered, "Bessie, now you do."

He deeded us five acres of land four miles outside Woodville, but on the opposite side of town from the fire tower. Frank and Elton came home to help clear the acres, and while stumps were still burning and brush fires smoldering, we arranged to have our house moved. That was a terrible time for Grandfather. He could not understand what was happening. While he was in bed, the movers arrived and jacked up the house. Then they loaded it onto a truck, and toward evening, they moved it no more than an eighth of a mile to the highway, where it sat overnight. The house was dangerously close to the road, and Mother insisted on tying Grandfather into his bed because he was prone to sleepwalking.

"Where are we, Daughter?" he asked.

Mother replied, "Oh, we're taking a little trip across town, that's all."

"But do we have to take our house with us?" he cried. "Why can't we stay where we were? Daughter, what have you done to us?"

Mother gave her father a very strong dose of cough medicine, and he slept quietly through the night, in spite of the cars whizzing past his bedroom windows.

The next morning at dawn the house movers arrived to transport us through Woodville, where the only traffic light in town hung so low over the intersection it had to be taken down before we could pass. Grandfather was still in a state of confusion, and no one could explain the situation to his satisfaction. When we arrived at the new location, the smoke and burning stumps gave him reason to believe he was soon to be cast into the fiery furnace of hell. "I don't believe we need to be here," he shouted. "Let's turn around. This place is too smoky."

Grandfather was unable to adjust to the new location. The smoke and dust aggravated his breathing. He wheezed and gasped for breath. At night he wandered in a half-sleep through the house or out into the yard, and someone would have to get up and guide him back to bed. Suddenly, his health, which was already precarious, declined even further, and our family doctor gave him only a few days to live. He said that Grandfather was suffering from consumption, which usually meant tuberculosis in those days, although that dreaded disease was never mentioned.

When word went out that Grandfather was dying, everyone came home to watch him go. His bedroom filled up with children, grandchildren, and friends. His sister, Rachel Durham, stood at the foot of his bed and rubbed his feet.

Great-Aunt Rachel was a Primitive Baptist. Her church observed the ceremony of foot washing, and she was forever trying to indoctrinate new members. After preaching a sermon, her minister would carry a pan of water into the congregation. He would then wash the feet of the first person on the first pew, and that person would take the pan of water and wash the feet of the next person, and so on and so forth, until every foot in the congregation sparkled.

"Jesus washed the feet of his disciples," Aunt Rachel said, "and that's why we wash each other's feet." She once told me that it made her very happy to have her feet washed and even happier to wash someone else's feet. The act of foot washing was very serious, and laughter during the rite made it even more serious. That was the way Aunt Rachel saw it. "There are times," she said, "when you just get beside yourself and can't stop laughing because getting your feet washed brings you closer to Jesus."

She did not wash Grandfather's feet on his death bed, but she did rub them until the very last. "Ain't that pretty up there," he kept saying while struggling for breath. "That's where I'm going." Many years later, Aunt Rachel told me that she was sorry she had not washed her dying brother's feet. "Maybe it would have made it a little easier for him if I had of," she said.

For me, being at Grandfather's deathbed was unbearable. His

breathing became more and more labored, and finally Aunt Bessie announced that he had the *death rattle.* "He doesn't have much time left," she told me, "so you better come up close to the bed so you can tell him good-bye before he goes to heaven."

At this point I escaped into the yard and distracted myself by watering the few patches of grass trying to take root in the sand. But my absence was noticed. Pretty soon Aunt Bessie came to the side porch and asked me to come inside again. "Papa's dying," she said. "Your place is inside with him until he goes."

I refused to leave the yard.

"Let him stay outside if he wants to," Mother said.

But no one else thought that watering the grass was proper behavior under the circumstances, so one by one aunts and uncles begged me to come inside. "Your grandfather is fighting for his life, and you're watering the grass," Uncle Frank shouted. "Pearl! Do something with that boy of yours."

Mother did nothing except to say once more, "Why don't you leave him alone."

Finally, they obeyed her, and I was left alone to water in peace. But in an hour or so I became curious. There were no voices wafting from Grandfather's bedroom and no movement in the air. The afternoon was still and breathless as if a glass bowl had been dropped over our house and yard. Wondering what was going on, I pressed my face against the window screen and saw everyone standing close to Grandfather's bed as if they expected him to say something important. But he was beyond words. Pearls were in his eyes. His lips were white. And one hand was slightly raised, a finger pointing upward in the direction he was soon to travel.

I stood there for some time until Uncle Frank pointed his finger at me. "Boy, you better come on inside, right now." I replied by

pointing the hose through the window and sprinkling the mourn-
ers with a stream of water that scattered them to the other side
of the room. Suddenly, the afternoon silence was broken. "Pearl,"
someone shouted, "do something with that boy. He'll turn out
bad for sure, if you don't." Uncle Frank took the garden hose away
from me and led me into Grandfather's bedroom. A few minutes
later, another restless calm descended upon us, and when it
seemed as though the entire world had lost its breath, Grandfather died with beads of water still on his face.

The Artist

UNCLE FRANK was a dragline operator who dredged a good portion of the Intracoastal Waterway. He also helped build roads and bridges in many states and considered himself a maverick. Often he boasted of living on the edge and wanted me to write the story of his life. A few months before he died, he asked me when I was going to get started. I think he must have sensed his time was almost up. We were standing in the Scribner Bookstore in New York, where I worked as a clerk. Frank, his last wife, and his two daughters were on their way to Brazil, where a construction company was sending him to build highways and bridges. I told him that it would be impossible for me to write his biography without writing about all his wives and lovers.

"So write about them," he said.

"Can you put them in chronological order?" I asked, and he replied:

"Hell, I can't even remember their names."

Grandmother was the only member of the family who possessed an ability to remember names, but only the names she would have been better off forgetting. Prone to self-torture, she would not allow herself to forget the names of Frank's painted women. "They," she predicted, "will be Frank's downfall. He couldn't pick a decent woman if his life depended on it; I guess he just can't recognize one."

"And I wonder why?" my mother asked with a sweet smile.

In his youth Frank was a tall man with tight, thin muscles, a shock of black, wavy hair, and a prominent nose giving his face a strong and desperate quality that women (and more than a few men) found irresistible. Sunburned and scarfaced, he gave the impression of traveling under a cloud of sex and danger. In spite of his macho image, he was just as comfortable in the kitchen as he was on a dragline. Unlike most men of his generation, he did not seem to distinguish between mopping the floors and operating a road grader. During many visits, he mopped our entire house until every particle of dust in every corner had been removed. "You need somebody to come in here and swab your decks, Sis," he would say. "You don't know how to keep house worth a damn." The next day he might be operating a bulldozer or washing his clothes by hand, ironing, fishing, hunting squirrel with a .22, or sewing on a button, repairing a zipper, a clock, a radio. Frank could do anything except sing and was known as the best cook in our family. No matter what he did, he gave himself to the task. A perfectionist of the worst kind, he was not only thorough, he was fast. He could do the work of five men, and he was never still, not for a minute, not even when he was drinking himself into a stupor in some Gulf Coast dive. He often came home from those "dens of iniquity," as Grandmother called them, with scratches, scars, and black eyes; once with a bullet wound in his leg.

The Gulf Coast was Frank's paradise. "Salt water's bad for your brain," Grandmother always said. "It'll rust out your car, and it'll rust out you." She thought the Texas Gulf Coast was a land of

Uncle Frank at Camp Ruby, early 1940s

immorality, a wall-to-wall brothel emitting a stench like none other. It was the only part of Texas Frank loved. He smelled of cigarettes, stale beer, and salt air, and to this day I cannot gaze upon the Gulf of Mexico without thinking of him.

"Frank," Grandmother said, "has been going up Fool's Hill all his life, and there's nothing anybody can do to stop him."

Grandmother hated all of Frank's wives and girlfriends. She called them Gulf Coast trash and said they were "sorry as dirt and belonged in the sewer." She could spit out their names with such vehemence the temperature in the house seemed to rise at an alarming rate.

"Hush," my mother would say. "You'll burn the house down talking that way, and then what will we do? Where will we go? The poor folks' home, I suppose."

Of all the women and wives Frank brought home, the one I remember most clearly was Jean. God only knows what happened to her. Grandmother swore that Jean was the bottom of the line and that Frank would never be able to sink any lower. In my opinion, Jean was the best. She was in her late twenties or early thirties when Frank brought her home the first time. I was no more than eight or nine years old, and she was the most exotic creature I'd ever seen up close. She drew heavy black lines around her eyelids. No one else in my family did this. She wore false eyelashes, blue and green eye shadow, and a beauty spot that traveled around her mouth from visit to visit. Her Maybelline eyebrows were nothing less than two black grease marks, and her lips and cheeks were painted as if for the stage.

Each time Frank brought her home the color of her hair was a little different. It was either platinum white, like paper napkins, or various shades of golden blond, at times almost yellow. It was coarse hair. "Like horse tail," Grandmother said. But it was not perfectly straight. It was rather wavy and held in place with black bobby pins and barrettes encrusted with rhinestones. The contrast between black bobby pins and shockingly blond hair was breathtaking.

Jean was a full-figured woman who reeked of cigarettes, bourbon, and Listerine. She often wore bandana blouses stretched to the limits across her breasts, and she had a predilection for tight skirts with small kick pleats, toreador pants, fishnet stockings, and high, high heels, either black or white. She was terribly theatrical and confessed to me in what my grandmother interpreted as "conspiratorial whispers" that she was involved in a leg of show business.

We were sitting on the porch swing when she volunteered this information about herself. It was a humid Sunday afternoon. Jean, resting an arm on my shoulder, said in a silky voice:

"I believe I can tell you this. Please, don't tell your mother or grandmother, but I am what you call a *striptease artist.*"

Artist was all I needed to hear. The very sound of the word produced such excitement I could hardly speak. I was sure that I was an artist too, but I had no idea what kind. How I admired Jean for knowing exactly what kind of artist she was.

That day she told me she was working on a new routine. She said that she was going to strip to a Beethoven symphony, I forget which one. Her intention was to personify the music with movement, to remove her clothes without anyone realizing what she had done. "At the end," she said, "I will stand before the audience, but I will not be naked. I will be *wearing* the music."

Unfortunately for me, Jean was on her way out of our house almost before she was allowed to enter. The first day Frank brought her home, Grandmother demanded to see their marriage license, and Frank, to everyone's surprise, produced one. On inspecting the license, Grandmother reluctantly agreed to allow them to sleep in the same bed.

In the middle of the night, Jean tiptoed into my grandmother's bedroom and gave her a big wake-up kiss on the cheek. "Can I call you Mom?" she asked. "I never had a mother of my own, and if I had to choose, I'd pick one just like you."

I don't know exactly what Grandmother said in reply, but whatever it was the message was clear: Jean was not allowed to spend the night under our roof ever again.

Still, Frank and Jean continued visiting us occasionally, usually for a few hours on a Saturday or Sunday afternoon, and I continued liking her more and more with each visit. She had a light-hearted spirit and enjoyed playing in the sand. Dressed in tight pedal pushers or straight skirts and blouses with plunging necklines, she would kick off her heels and sit with me on the wet ground. Together we created some impressive sand castles. But I must admit, she did most of the creating herself. With both hands in the dirt or a bucket of water, she would spend hours constructing a fantastic castle where, one day, she hoped to reside.

She would mold the sand into forms I could never have imagined, and on hot summer days when no breeze was stirring, her very presence was intoxicating. Often I was unable to take my eyes off her—her magnificent breasts shining through her thin blouse, her beaded eyelashes and blue-green lids, her pancake makeup as thick as peanut butter, and, of course, that hair, those yellow or napkin-white curls sparkling with imagination and glass jewels. Along with grains of sand embedded in her cleavage, she wore the allure of seduction as easily as she wore her fishnet hose or her favorite perfume, Evening in Paris. On warm nights, that dime-store fragrance would linger in our house and yard long after Frank and Jean had departed for some nearby motel.

"You can't get rid of trash such as that," my grandmother would grumble. "The dirt is where all of Frank's women belong." She called Jean the Painted Whore of Babylon. But Jean called herself an artist, and as far as I was concerned, she was exactly that.

The Stolen Television Set

IN THE EARLY 1950s Uncle Frank brought home a television set. Grandmother was convinced he had stolen it. She relegated the set to a back room and threatened to deliver it to the city dump in the dead of night. Somehow we managed to keep it.

During those days television was live. *Hallmark Hall of Fame* delivered Broadway plays to our doorsteps. Leonard Bernstein conducted concerts for children. *Omnibus* and *Producer's Showcase* presented dramas both classical and modern, and *The Ed Sullivan Show* exposed us to a variety of performing artists, among them Lily Pons. She usually sang the "Bell Song," the "Shadow Song," or some other coloratura showstopper while my grandmother covered her ears and screamed, "Who can stand that racket? A woman with a voice like that ought to be shot in the head."

Then one day I turned on the television set and the Indian ballerina, Maria Tallchief, came leaping into our living room. I believe she may have been costumed as the Firebird. Whatever it was, Maria Tallchief changed my life. Until then, I had never seen anything quite like ballet. To my young Texas eyes, it was the most exotic spectacle I had ever witnessed. At that time I didn't know what a *piqué* turn was. I didn't know a pirouette from a *rond de jambe,* but with a few books from the library I soon learned. Overnight balletomania struck, and it has turned into an incurable, not to mention expensive, state of being; some might even call it a mental illness—my grandmother certainly did.

During the early 1950s ballet was on television quite a lot. I would sit inches from the screen and try to remember every step while Grandmother grumbled in the background. She hated ballet. "Look at the bitch hiking up her legs," she would shout. "A woman like that ought to be poisoned."

She thought that a person would have to be crazy to dance ballet and even crazier to sit down and watch it. "Don't try to make me believe you're enjoying it," she said. "Because I, for one, won't believe you. Don't try to make me believe it's pretty, because I already know it's not, and don't go out of your way to pretend you're getting something out of it for I'm not as gullible as I look."

No matter what she said, her words made no dent on me, and before long I was telling everyone:

"I'm going to be a ballerina just like Maria Tallchief."

No one paid much attention to my growing aspiration until I stuffed my moccasins with nylon stockings in order to walk *en pointe*. For my practice sessions, which took place in the living room or lawn, I wore a green wool skirt and a T-shirt, a costume I never wanted to remove. Grandmother swore that it was going to rot on me. And it almost did. How proud I was to balance without a wobble or pirouette without falling on my face. I never mastered double pirouettes, only single ones, and the Swan Queen's required thirty-two fouettés were, from my point of view, a miraculous achievement forever beyond my capability, but that did not stop me from practicing and showing off. When Mother went into Woodville to shop, I, in my ballerina outfit, would tag right along. In and out of the dress shops, the post office, the court-house, and all along the streets, I would dance behind her like the Lilac Fairy—always *en pointe*.

"I sure am glad I don't have to go up there and witness it," Grandmother said, "for I might turn red. Pearl, why do you allow him to do these things, that's what I'd like to know? Why do you just stand there while he makes a fool out of himself and all the rest of us?"

I can't recall Mother answering either of these questions. If she saw anything embarrassing about my aspiration, she did not show it. But the townspeople were of a different mind. One day when Mother was shopping in Mr. Pate's grocery store and I was dancing behind her on my toes, Mrs. Pate leaned over the counter and said in a rather condescending tone: "Pearl, who's that pretty little girl you've got with you?" Without hesitation, my Mother answered proudly:

"That's my son."

For Mother, the most disconcerting thing about my ambition was my growing proficiency at *pointe* work. She was afraid that I would ruin my feet, and I almost did. I suffered blisters, bruises, and split toenails, and still I continued dancing until my feet were so mangled I could hardly walk without a limp. Only then did I abandon my dancing shoes, but not my love of ballet. I watched every ballet, opera, and drama on television while Grandmother complained bitterly about something she called my *proclivity*.

She was convinced that the television was introducing detri-mental ideas into our home, and what was worse, the set wasn't even ours. "It doesn't belong to us," she harped. "We didn't buy it, and we didn't ask for it, and we don't want it. One day some-body will come along and claim it. One day we'll all go to jail because of Frank. Because of that damn television set, we'll be thrown into the penitentiary."

Finally, she accepted the presence of the television set in our house and even came to enjoy it, but only after she had read her way through the public library and had nothing else to occupy her ever-wandering mind.

Grandmother could read three or four books a day and often did, but not once did she go to the library herself. "I might scare somebody if I go up there," she said. Over and over she told us that she was the ugliest person who ever walked the earth and for that reason she had no intention of being seen in public. "Nobody wants to look at somebody like me," she grumbled. "My nose is too long. I can't wear my teeth. My clothes are rags. Pearl! Will you go get me a book. Pearl, I need something else to read right now. Pearl, you'll have to go up there and find me something. You know I can't go out looking like I do."

I can't say that Grandmother was ugly, but she certainly wasn't a raving beauty either. What comely features she may have had were dramatically upstaged by an unusually large humpback nose. It was so long she could touch the end of it with her tongue, a trick she seemed to enjoy performing. Naturally, this did little to enhance what beauty she possessed and provoked some of her grandchildren to refer to her as a crazy old witch.

In Camp Ruby her appearance never seemed to bother her. But in Woodville, she was painfully self-conscious about her features. Of course, it is possible, and even probable, that her "ugly" diatribes were a way of controlling all of us. She did love to be waited on hand over foot. And she did enjoy sending Mother running to the library. Back and forth she would go carrying armloads of books, few of which met Grandmother's approval.

Finally, Mother put her foot down. "I've had enough of this," she said. And from then on, I was in charge of choosing Grandmother's reading material. We were already bringing home every magazine and newspaper on the rack, but she ripped through them in no time. What she wanted was books and more books. Big thick books. Interesting books. Books that would tell her something she didn't already know. And since she already knew *everything*, it was impossible to please her, particularly when her interests turned to crime.

Before long she had read every detective story and murder mystery in the Woodville library, and she wanted more, more, more. I would bring home a stack of books, and one by one she would throw them on the floor or against the wall. "I've already read that," she would say, not in anger but in disappointment. "I've already read that, too. I've read that, and that, and that." I'd then pick up the books, and Mother would get ready to drive me back to the library.

"Please," Grandmother would beg, "please, bring me something I haven't already read."

"But Grandmother," I would argue, "I can't remember what you've read and what you haven't read."

"Well *try*," she would say, as if no one had ever tried to please her. "Just *try* for once in your life to find a book I haven't read, and make it a detective story, one I can't figure out."

The problem was, she could figure all of them out. She had a mind for sleuthing through facts and recognizing a perpetrator of crime. Everything we brought home was too easy for her, especially Agatha Christie. "I can see straight through that idiot," she said. "Why would anybody want to read her?" She was repulsed by Miss Marple because she was a *silly old woman* and was disgusted by Poirot because he was a *fancy little man.* She loved Sherlock Holmes, however. She loved him passionately, while hating Sir Arthur Conan Doyle because he had not written enough books to satisfy her demand.

On realizing that we were right, that there was nothing left in the public library for her to read, Grandmother turned to crossword puzzles, but as might be expected, all were too easy for her. She would solve them in a flash and then be desperate for something else to do. Before long she started making shag rugs from nylon stockings, but this too did not occupy every corner of her restless mind, so she turned to gathering hickory nuts, cracking them, and picking them out for eating and baking. She said it was the hardest nut in the world to crack, and the challenge of digging out every tiny particle of meat from the intricate shell gave her something to do. Although she may have tired of these activities she kept pursuing them, and finally, out of sheer desperation, if nothing else, she turned on the *stolen* television set and got hooked on wrestling.

Overnight Grandmother fell in love with Gorgeous George, a beefy blond wrestler popular in the fifties. She lived for wrestling matches and would sit with her little wrinkled face only inches from the snowy screen and root for her hero.

"Will somebody bring me my sugar," she would shout. "I can't get up right now." She called her snuff "sugar," but she also called hard candy "sugar" as well. If we brought her one instead of the other she would scream, "That's the wrong kind of sugar!" You just had to know instinctively what she was talking about and bring the right thing at the right time, especially during wrestling matches. There she would sit indulging herself in a newfound passion while brown sugar dribbled from the corners of her mouth and white sugar settled into her diabetic feet.

"Mama's got a boyfriend," Mother said. "And his name is Gorgeous George."

Grandmother replied, "What does somebody like you know about boyfriends?"

"What does somebody like you know about wrestling?" Mother snapped back, and Grandmother set her straight: "I've got eyes. I can see. I can put two and two together. I know it's a fake, but I like it anyway. So what?"

Because wrestling was televised only two or three times a week, Grandmother was left with quite a lot of free time. She would flip from one of our three channels to another with such aggressive wrist motion it was a wonder the knob wasn't ripped right off the set. By flipping back and forth, she discovered country music programs that she liked quite a lot, particularly Curly Fox and Texas Ruby, a husband and wife duo. "They're probably degenerates," she said, "but they sure can sing." She also discovered the Houston news reports. They were violent and bloody, and that suited her just fine. All at once, her interest in criminology returned like a tornado.

"Everybody's being murdered in Houston," she said. "Nobody's safe there anymore. Everybody's being shot or stabbed or thrown in the river. We never lost anything in that town so there's no reason for any of us to go there looking for it. Everybody better be staying out of Houston, and that includes Frank too."

For several days she would study a crime intensely. She would listen to the news reports, peruse daily papers, and absorb herself in all the facts and clues. Then she would go off inside herself, mull it all over, and emerge with her findings:

"I believe I know where the body's buried. Why doesn't someone come ask me what I know? I believe the son-in-law's in on it. I believe the husband's not what he seems. Maybe he has a previous record. Maybe he has another name. Maybe he has a foolproof disguise. Wouldn't surprise me. Pearl, come give me your opinion. Pearl, come tell me what you think about all this."

"I stopped thinking a long time ago," my Mother would reply, and Grandmother would answer:

"Yes, and that's just one of your problems, and Frank's not far behind you, if any at all."

Every time she heard about a new crime Grandmother would say, "I wonder where Frank is right now. I sure hope he's not involved in this tangled up mess."

Four times a day, morning, noon, evening, and night, she watched the news telecasts and wondered if the day would ever come when she would hear her son's name mentioned over the air. "He's going to end up in the pen," she told us over and over. "I just know he is."

The more she absorbed herself in armchair criminology, the more she was convinced: "Frank's heading for trouble. He's about to have a run-in with the law." She would say this as if she were a teary-eyed Cassandra, lamenting all the way: "Nobody will believe me until it happens, but it's true, true, true. You can't go around grabbing things that don't belong to you and never get caught. One day your number will come up. One day your luck will run out. One day the cards will turn against you."

Frank's Run-in with the Law

I N 1954, Frank's luck ran out. He was sent to Camden, Arkansas, with a team of bridge builders and had been there just long enough for the owner of the local liquor store to know him by name. Frank was a regular customer, personable and full of fun, but hot-tempered. One night he staggered into the store to buy a bottle of whisky. He was already drunk to begin with, and the owner, realizing this, refused to sell him anything. "I can't take your money tonight, Frank," the man said. "You need to go home and sleep it off." But Frank was not accustomed to being refused. He lost his temper, stormed out of the store, and a few minutes later he returned with a sawed-off shotgun. Pointing it in the owner's face, he made off with no more than fifty dollars and a few bottles of whisky. Almost immediately he was apprehended and thrown into jail.

I don't remember who Frank was married to or living with at the time, but whoever she was, Grandmother blamed her for Frank's run-in with the law.

When the bad news reached us by telephone, Grandmother went all to pieces. "May the dear Lord take me tonight," she cried. "Frank's out to disgrace us in the eyes of the entire human race. That's all he studies about."

She decided that there was only one thing to do: drive under cover of night to Arkansas, spring Frank from jail, and return without anyone realizing we had left town. This was her reasoning: "When the good people of Camden, Arkansas, see what a decent family Frank comes from they'll know right away that a mistake has been made and let him go. Then we can bring him home and get him started on the right foot."

She was afraid that all of Tyler County was going to find out about Frank's trouble. "Don't you dare go up to that school house and tell all your little friends what your uncle has done," she said to me. "And don't tell Old Lady Woodcock either."

Mrs. Margaret Woodcock was our neighbor who lived a quarter of a mile down the road. She was a plump, auburn-haired woman in her early sixties who wore homemade dresses, many of them with princess necklines. Safety-pinned to the waist or bodice of each dress was a hairnet that she twisted obsessively with one or both hands to calm her nerves and restless mind. Mrs. Woodcock had been married five times. She had outlived four husbands and had means of finding out everything that happened in Tyler County. Snooping was her passion. We were on the same party line, and she undoubtedly spent a lot of time eavesdropping, but she also made regular visits to the city dump to rummage through the discarded substance of other people's lives. I usually accompanied her. We would collect old clothes, rags, and sacks of letters, all of which she read and reread with the greatest interest, and so did her husband Leo. Leo was a barber. Every day he came home for lunch and brought the latest news he had heard in his shop, so between the two of them, they eventually uncovered every skeleton in every closet.

Grandmother was determined that Mrs. Woodcock should never find out about Frank's incarceration. By leaving for Arkansas late one night and coming back the next day, our nosy

Mrs. Margaret Woodcock

neighbor would not be too likely to miss us, or so my grand-mother thought.

Seven of us made the eight-hour trip in Mother's two-door Ford. Grandmother and Aunt Coleta rode in the front seat. I rode in the back with Sissie, Clinton, and Mur. Mother, behind the wheel, chain-smoked the entire way. Sissie, whose crinolines filled up most of the back seat, chewed Juicy Fruit gum while her father and brother chewed tobacco and our grandmother dipped her sugar and spat into a tin can. Along the way Aunt Coleta chattered incessantly about her poor brother, who was born not knowing what foot to stand on. Now and again she hushed for a moment or two while Grandmother reminded us that our purpose was to make a favorable impression on everybody we met in the state of Arkansas.

We arrived tired and cranky, wrinkled and stiff, and were not allowed, by Grandmother's edict, to stop at a motel and freshen up. "Motels cost money," she said, "we can primp in the car and look just as good." In accordance with her command, we went straight to the county jail to rescue Frank. "All he needs," she announced, "is for somebody to take care of him. That's what I'm here for."

The jailhouse was a stone building of two or three stories surrounded by a lawn and shrubbery. A flight of stairs led to a small porch several feet off the ground. The jailer's wife guided us up an inside staircase to a large communal cell where three or four lawbreakers, Frank among them, were locked up. He stood behind a steel door and talked to us through a small barred window. His long nose protruded through the bars and made Sissie laugh.

No one knew what to say to Frank, and he certainly didn't know what to say to us. We were standing, all seven of us, on a small landing that could barely hold four people. Grandmother, choking on her words, ended up crying while the rest of us tried to comfort her. Suddenly, Frank turned his attention to me.

"What's that you're wearing around your neck?" he asked.

"A western tie," I answered. "Do you want it?"

"No," he replied. "They won't let me have anything like that in jail. They're afraid I might use it to choke somebody."

Hearing this, Grandmother began sobbing loudly: "Frankie's a good boy, he wouldn't choke anybody unless he had to." Sissie and Aunt Coleta echoed her, while Mother, leaning against a wall, smoked aggressively but did not speak, and Clinton and Mur swayed from foot to foot.

Alarmed by the commotion, the jailer hurried up the stairs to calm everyone down. When he informed us that Frank would have to stand trial and there was no way out of it, Grandmother began losing control. "We're a fine family," she cried. "We deserve better treatment than this. We're decent people whether anybody in this town realizes it or not."

Then Frank received a telephone call. "It's one of your sorry women, isn't it?" Grandmother asked. "Which one is it this time?"

Frank didn't answer. The jailer unlocked the cell and shackled one of Frank's legs with a ball and chain that he dragged downstairs to the phone. That iron ball, crashing against each step, rattled every nerve in Grandmother's body. She stood there with her head bowed, biting what was left of her lips and blowing her nose. Her entire body trembled. "I need some sugar," she said, pulling hard candy from the bodice of her dress.

"Mama, did you take your insulin?" Aunt Coleta asked.

Grandmother replied sharply: "You know I didn't have time, why do you even ask such a thing?" She put a piece of candy in her mouth and leaned against the wall with her eyes closed. She stayed that way, snapping her purse open and shut, until Frank was returned to his cell. At that time, Grandmother, still trembling all over, wanted to know who had called. "It was some no count woman, wasn't it? I don't know why you can't admit it." Frank answered with a labored smile and Grandmother cried: "I knew it was. You can't fool me on these things."

Weeping uncontrollably, she went careening down the stairs. Sissie and I followed close behind. We begged her not to cry. We told her everything would be all right. We said whatever we could think of to comfort her, but by then words were useless. She went thrashing through the jailer's office and out the front door to the high porch. Then suddenly, before my cousin and I had actually seen what had happened, our grandmother went flying over the banister. Did she jump? Did she merely trip and decide to pitch herself forward? To this day we have no idea what really happened, or what Grandmother's intention might have been, but this much we know:

She was airborne forever.

In an instant she had taken to the air, hovering above the lawn as if she had sprouted wings. Her long hair came out of its bun and puffed out all over her head. Her purse went sailing across the yard, as did Kleenex, dipping snuff, and loose change. Hard candy flew from her brassiere and fell like hailstones on the sidewalk. It seemed as though time had stopped or slowed down and that our grandmother would never fall, that she would just go on flying over the lawn forever.

True to character, Sissie began laughing hysterically, even when Grandmother landed on her side with a heavy thud. She rolled over and over, but never once did she make a sound, not a whimper, not a moan, and not even one word of foul language spewed from her lips. She lay there as still as a mouse while Sissie continued laughing, and Frank, looking down from his barred window called out, "Mother, I didn't go to do it."

What Sissie remembers most clearly about that day was a midget standing on the sidewalk observing the scene with detachment. I don't remember the midget myself, but Sissie swears he was there, and that Uncle Frank screamed at him: "Don't just stand there, you tiny little son of a bitch. Go pick up my Mother before I send somebody down there to beat the shit out of you."

If Sissie says the midget was there, I am sure he was and that he did not move a muscle or register the slightest reaction. For that matter, neither did Grandmother. She lay on the lawn and was perfectly still. For all we knew she was dead, but of course, she wasn't. Within a few minutes an ambulance arrived to take her to the local hospital. The rest of us followed on foot while Sissie continued laughing. I don't remember Mother saying anything. She lagged far behind the rest of us, as if she wanted no association with this fine family from the state of Texas, while Mur and Clinton, also reticent, took the lead. At some point along the way to the hospital we stopped at a drugstore to buy something and the cashier received an earful.

"Lord help us," Aunt Coleta told the woman ringing up our sales. "Here we are hundreds of miles away from home. We don't have no money. We don't have no fresh clothes, and we don't know nobody living in this town except my brother Frank and *you've* got him locked up. Now Mama's tried to kill herself, and we don't have the slightest idea what to do next."

As well as suffering bruises and scratches, Grandmother broke a shoulder and an arm. Because of her age, the doctors in Camden refused to set her bones. Instead, they transferred her to a specialist in Little Rock. Aunt Coleta accompanied her in an ambulance while the rest of us followed in Mother's Ford. Along the way we had a blowout, which delayed our arrival, and by the time we made it to the Little Rock hospital Grandmother was wearing several plaster casts and sporting a new hairdo. While she had been sedated, a young, energetic, and very pretty black nurse had plaited her long hair into dozens of tiny braids with a bow ribbon of every color tied to the end of each one.

"Get that goddamn little nigra out of my room before I kill her," Grandmother was shouting when we arrived. "I won't have her messing with my hair anymore."

"You have the sweetest little grandmother," the nurse replied. "She'll let me do anything I want to her hair."

"I will not," Grandmother screamed. "Get that sorry little bitch out of my room." But the nurse displayed nothing but amusement over her patient's prejudice and distress. "How did somebody like you get to be so sweet?" she would say while Grandmother growled and hissed.

The next day we returned home. Mrs. Woodcock must have been watching the highway because the moment we entered the house she telephoned to say, "You didn't tell me you were taking a vacation." Grandmother told her we had been visiting Frank and left it at that, but Mrs. Woodcock knew there was more. Her eyes fairly danced out of her head when she saw bruises and plaster casts. With both hands twisting her hair net, she asked Grandmother what had happened but received no answer.

In a few months Frank was sentenced to four years in the Arkansas state prison. "May the dear Lord take me tonight," my grandmother said when the news reached her. During his incarceration he wrote to Grandmother several times a week, and slowly our curious neighbor pieced the story together. One day, a few years after Frank had been released, Mrs. Woodcock and I were fishing on the river. Out of the blue she said to me, "I wonder why your grandmother didn't burn those letters of Frank's that time he got into trouble?" I offered no explanation. Nor did I acknowledge that I had even heard her. But to this day, Mrs. Woodcock's question has puzzled me. Grandmother knew that our neighbor perused the city dumping grounds. I was often with her rooting through old suitcases and bags of clothing, looking for anything of interest. It was our greatest pastime. Knowing this, why did Grandmother cast Frank's letters upon the city dumping grounds to be found by whomever happened along? Surely there must have been some degree of intention in her decision not to shred those letters or burn them in the backyard, or safer still, in the kitchen sink.

Frank's Death and Funeral

AFTER FRANK was released from prison he returned home to live. He kept himself busy repairing the roof and reading the Bible. He kept his hair combed, his face shaved, and made a point of wearing a clean set of clothes every day. Grandmother said he was making a complete about-face. After six weeks, however, he became restless and struck out for the Gulf Coast again. In the next ten years he married several times, once to a woman who bore him two daughters, and for who knows what reason, shot him in the leg. Within a few weeks of the shooting Frank divorced her. Grandmother said it was the smartest thing he had ever done, but before long he disappointed her by marrying yet again.

About that time, he was sent to Brazil with a construction team. He was happy to take his family with him, but after a few months he got tired of his new wife and sent her back to the United States. Shortly thereafter, he suffered a fatal heart attack. He was only fifty-five years old, and his daughters were with him.

The daughters returned to the States at once, but only after Frank's company had navigated oceans of red tape did the Brazilian authorities agree to release the body. Several days after agreements had been signed and sealed, there arrived at the Pace Funeral Home in

Livingston, Texas, the most spectacular black coffin anyone had ever seen. Instantly, everyone in town knew about it. The coffin was made of wood, ornately carved and lacquered. "It looks just like a coffin is supposed to look, the shape and all," Sissie exclaimed. "Even if you'd never before seen one, you'd know what you're looking at."

People who had never known Frank, or even heard of him, drove for miles just to look at his fancy casket. Not only was it elaborately carved, it was completely sealed with screws. On top, however, was an opening about six inches square covered with plate glass and a small hinged door, also elaborately carved. Aunt Coleta was one of the first to lift the lid. She pressed a flashlight against the window and turned it on. "Lord have mercy," she cried. "They didn't even wash his face! Don't let Pearl look at him for she will never sleep a night if she does. Don't let Pearl look at him, for she'll never be able to eat another bite nor even draw a breath."

Frank had died in bed, and the Brazilian authorities sealed him up in the coffin without changing his clothes. He was still wearing pajamas. His face was bloody and his hair uncombed. "For God's sake," Aunt Coleta cried. "It's a disgrace. Don't anybody let Pearl lift that lid. You know how upset she gets over death. It's been hard enough for her to get over Big Eddie. Who knows what would become of her if she was forced to look at Frank in the shape he's in."

"I want to see my brother," Mother kept saying. But every time she approached the coffin to open the lid, someone stopped her. "I just want to say good-bye," she cried, but still no one would allow her to look at Frank. After his burial, she kept saying, "I just want to see my brother one more time."

Within a week she got her wish.

Mother and I were driving through the town of Livingston. She was behind the wheel. At the red light we stopped behind a delivery truck that seemed to be stalled there. A man who looked exactly like Frank got out on the driver's side and stood in the middle of the street. He just stood there staring at Mother as if he were about to speak or call her name. He had Frank's long nose, Frank's sunburned complexion, Frank's tiny eyes and sly smile. He had Frank's black, wavy hair, Frank's hands, Frank's chipped teeth and tall lean stature. Everything about him was *Frank.*

"There's my brother," Mother screamed. "There's Frank!"

As soon as she spoke he moved. He walked forward. His eyes were fixed on Mother. Then he gave her a big smile, walked to the other side of the truck, and got in. The light changed. Another driver took over and the truck moved on. But we stayed put. We were in no condition to move. Finally, Mother parked at the curb, and we sat there for quite some time before we were able to continue on our way.

In the few years remaining in her life, we rarely spoke of that experience, and when we did we knew better than to linger over it. We would sometimes say, "Do you remember the day we saw Frank?" knowing all the while that the other remembered—for how could it be forgotten?—but also knowing that we needed to say something about the experience without destroying it, to reassure the other that what we had seen had indeed been seen and not dreamed.

Frank's spirit returned to say good-bye to Mother. It is as simple and complex as that. A few years later, only minutes after her death, in fact, Mother said good-bye to me.

I'm certain it was no dream.

Elizabeth Ann, Called Sissie

S ISSIE ONCE SAID that it's hard to tell if you're dreaming or not until you wake up and even then you're not always sure about it; so what is a dream anyway?

When we were growing up I don't recall her ever dreaming about anything except becoming a beautician and owning her own parlor. "There's only one thing that worries me," she said. "Around here you'd be called on to fix up dead people, and I don't believe I could do that."

Still, she held to her ambition as long as possible by practicing on every living soul around including herself. She was always trying to straighten hair or curl hair, make thin lips appear voluptuous and voluptuous lips a little less so. She was constantly fooling with different kinds of mascara, brushes, powder puffs, and eyebrow pencils, which she moistened on the tip of her tongue. She also had a fetish for tweezers and still does. In her early teens she tweezed her eyebrows to a thin line and beyond. Hardly a hair was left when she got through, and today she has no eyebrows to speak of. She also used Mother's eyelash curler with enthusiasm to spare and ended up pulling every lash out of both lids. Fortunately, Sissie did not become a beautician.

While still dreaming of the day she would own a

beauty shop, she sometimes practiced makeup and hairstyles by drawing on her high school photographs. She used a fountain pen to reshape her lips, line her eyes, and redo her hair. She gave herself perfectly arched eyebrows and just as many lashes as she wanted.

Quite frequently, Sissie even practiced hard-earned beauty secrets on our grandmother, and from time to time, she asked me to assist. Because Grandmother was the kind of reckless diabetic who consumed anything that had sugar in it or sprinkled on top of it, she was often ill and spent a lot of time in bed sleeping. She was a very sound sleeper, and after Uncle Frank was sent to prison, Grandmother, consumed by humiliation and grief, seemed to be intent on sleeping the rest of her life away. Often it was hard to wake her up, and several times we thought she had drifted into a coma.

One afternoon when Grandmother was in a deep sleep, Sissie said to me, "Eddie Jr., let's go experiment on Grandmother. She looks like she's died on us, so let's fix up her face so she'll be real pretty the way she'll look in her coffin."

While Grandmother slept, we quite thoroughly painted her face. We gave her red cheeks, red lips, beauty marks, and eyebrows. When she woke up and wandered into the living room, everyone laughed. "Those goddamn kids," she said, "they've painted my face, haven't they?"

In spite of our practical jokes, Grandmother would enlist Sissie and me to comb her long hair until she fell asleep in her chair. She said that having her hair combed was the most relaxing thing in the world. For the most part, I was content to stand there and comb, but Sissie was not. She always felt obligated to do something special to Grandmother's hair.

One day after we had painted Grandmother's face, she begged to have her hair combed. I took the first shift and when I gave out, Sissie relieved me. Within a few minutes she became bored with combing and began experimenting with hairstyles she had read about. She created a very high pompadour, sausage curls, spit curls, finger waves, and who knows what else. "Grandmother!" she exclaimed, before the hair spray had settled, "I believe I've outdone myself today." Grandmother looked at herself in the mirror and said, "Nobody ought to be that ugly."

"Don't worry, Grandmother," Sissie said. "We're not through yet." Turning our attention to Grandmother's swollen feet, we painted her toenails bright red, at which time Sissie informed me: "Eddie Jr., I think we've gone about as far as we can go for one day. It's time to let Grandmother rest a little bit."

While she was still sporting her new hair, face, and brightly painted toenails, she settled into an easy chair and began reading one of her romance magazines, but before long her story was interrupted by someone knocking at the front door. Our visitor was a well-dressed, wealthy, and mild-mannered lady from the First Baptist Church who had come to enlist Grandmother in an extension Sunday school class. The lady was accompanied by her slightly retarded son, who was about twelve or thirteen years old. He was carrying a cap pistol on his belt, and he would go on carrying a cap pistol on his belt straight through high school and whatever followed. When Grandmother answered the door, the boy laughed and shot her in the face. She was not amused but refrained from expressing herself. The boy's mother took one look at Grandmother and several steps backward. "Oh!" she said in a nervous voice. "Maybe we better come back some other time."

Cousin Sissie, 1956, after touching herself up with a fountain pen

"Oh no," Grandmother replied, "come right in and sit down. We're not very busy today."

Hesitantly, the woman came in and sat down, and within a few minutes she and Grandmother were chattering away. They discussed the Bible, which Grandmother had read many times and could also quote when she felt like it, and that afternoon she did. While they discussed the latest Sunday school lesson, which Grandmother had not read but could discuss just the same, the lady's son sat on the floor sucking on his cap pistol and making disturbing sounds with his mouth. Not once did she correct him, and not once did she look Grandmother in the face. She stole uncomfortable sidelong glances. She took deep breaths. Her fingers danced across her bodice and neck, and she struggled to find her next word while Grandmother sat there with perfect equanimity, her hands folded in her lap, her crooked nose high in the air, and one foot placed on top of the other, her only attempt to hide her painted toes. As if she were the Queen of Sheba, she held forth for quite some time. She spouted Scripture and discussed local crimes, the cost of groceries, and the hideous fashions of the day, but not once did she apologize for, or comment on, her startling appearance.

"I hate you damn kids for that," she said after the lady and her son had left. "That's the last time you'll ever get a chance to humiliate me." A few days later Sissie was combing Grandmother's hair again, and Grandmother was dozing off in her chair. Whenever Sissie wanted to play beauty parlor games, Grandmother was always willing to be a customer.

FINALLY, Sissie abandoned her ambition to attend beauty school. Because of circumstances she has come to view her life as that of a caregiver. Many times she has volunteered to take care of the aged and the infirm, including her husband's relatives as well as her own parents, my mother, and Mother's brother Elton. If anyone needs help Sissie is the first to lend a hand. She believes that caring for people, particularly the aged, is one of her missions in life, along with discovering dead bodies. These discoveries have been sobering experiences to say the least, and today Sissie will rarely attend a funeral. "I've already done my part," she will say. "I can't look at another body."

After she found Uncle Elton dead in his trailer house, she said to me, "Eddie Jr., I've found more dead people than anybody I know. It looks to me like that's what I've been put here for, but I sure hope I don't have to find another one."

Uncle Elton's death seems to have disturbed her the most, and to this day she is still talking about it.

Elton made a career of the army. He did not come home as often as his brother, Frank, and for that reason we did not know him nearly as well until the very end of his life. After retiring, he married a woman from the state of Georgia, and they lived in a small town outside Atlanta. One day, seemingly for no reason at all, Elton shot his son-in-law's German shepherd dog. Then he opened fire on the son-in-law's house. He was arrested, thrown into jail, and because no one pressed charges he was given an ultimatum: stay in Georgia and stay in jail or leave the state and never return. Elton moved back to the state of Texas, which was glad to have him.

By then Sissie had married a man called Butch and was living next door to Mother on the property Mr. Carter had given us. Frank had already died, and Sissie was raising his two daughters. Although there was room for Elton in Mother's house, he preferred to live in a mobile home behind her garden and spend most of his time with Sissie and Butch. He never seemed to trust Mother. I think he suspected that she knew too much about him, and of course, she did.

While stationed in Germany, Elton lived with a woman who wrote to Grandmother frequently. Once she sent pictures of herself and a small child. In one of the pictures she was wearing nothing but a slip. "Cheap German Trash," Grandmother said. "That's what her name is."

Everyone suspected the child was Elton's, but no one ever questioned him on this touchy subject except Mother. One day she happened upon a picture of the German woman and the child. She showed the photograph to Frank's teenage daughters and said, "Next time Elton comes over here, I'm going to put this picture down beside him and see what he says."

A few days later Uncle Elton showed up for afternoon coffee, and Mother called Frank's daughters to come over and witness her plan in action. When the girls arrived, Mother served her brother a cup of coffee with the photograph resting like a cookie on the saucer. "Elton," Mother said, "do you know who this is?" Uncle Elton reacted as if he had touched a live wire. He called Mother every name he could think of. He told her she was mean and conniving and Mother replied, "Oh, I see you *do* recognize this precious child after all." Then she turned to Frank's children and said. "You girls have a little cousin in Germany. You better go looking for him. He might be worth a lot of money."

After that Elton avoided Mother. He made a point of asking how she was feeling before coming over, but he never lingered in her presence long enough for a cup of coffee. He said he didn't like Mother's coffee anyway. He said it was too bitter—just like her. He also said that her cooking was worse, and that he would never eat a bite at her house for fear of being poisoned. He preferred Sissie's cooking. "Now there's a cook," he said. "Sissie understands food."

Sissie has always been a traditional southern cook. Her meals are heavy in fried meats, usually chicken, beef, pork, venison, catfish, frog legs, or squirrel. Vegetables are thoroughly boiled and everything is sugared, salted, and peppered. Greens are seasoned with fatback and hamburgers are fried through and through. Nothing is left undercooked. Because of her remarkable ability in menu planning and food preparation, she has often been called into service at local hospitals, schools, and retirement homes. With seven loaves of bread and a few little catfish, she too can feed a multitude. Waste not, want not is her way of thinking. She knows how to stretch a bean and will.

No one else in the family possesses her remarkable touch in the kitchen, and if Uncle Elton were alive today, he would still be saying, "I'd rather eat Sissie's cooking than anybody's." While he lived next door, he took at least three meals a day with her, and during that time he gained quite a bit of weight. He was particularly fond of hot dogs, and Sissie prepared them often. Garnished with mustard, mayonnaise, chopped onions, pickle relish, and smothered with chili con carne, jalapeño peppers, and mountains of grated rat cheese, a single hot dog was a meal in itself. But Uncle Elton, being a tall man with a big appetite, was not satisfied with a single hot dog. He could eat as many as Sissie could prepare.

Late one afternoon, when she was out of the house and Elton

was attacked with hunger pangs, he decided to raid the refrigerator. There he found two packages of hot dogs and ate them both in one sitting. Shortly after that, Sissie came home to prepare supper. "I fixed him two pairs of frog legs and a plate of French fries," she remembers, "but he said he wasn't hungry, and that wasn't like him. He said he'd take it home and eat it before he went to bed, and that's what he did."

The next morning she heard the hum of Uncle Elton's air conditioner and wondered if something was wrong. Because he was tight with his money and didn't want to run up an electric bill, he never burned the air conditioner all night long. With this in mind, Sissie decided to go see about him.

After knocking on the door several times, she broke the lock and went inside. The frog legs and French fries had been eaten. The dirty plates were in the sink and Uncle Elton was still in bed, where he had died of gastric indigestion.

That was almost twenty years ago, but to hear Sissie talk it could have been yesterday. "Two pair of frog legs and a plate of French fries sure won't hurt you," she continues to say. "So it must have been the weenies that killed him. Two packages is too much for any one person to eat all by himself."

In some strange way she holds herself partially accountable for Elton's death. "I have never told anybody when to stop eating," she has said many times. "If it's on my table and you want it, it's yours to eat, but I sure do wish I had been at home to take just one package of weenies away from Uncle Elton. He might have lived if I had."

Now and then, when it's just the two of us, Sissie's eyes will cloud over and her mouth will droop. Suddenly she will say, "Eddie Jr., after Uncle Elton ate himself to death, I just can't stand to look at a weenie anymore, can you? I believe it would kill me if I was forced to eat one."

UNTIL RECENTLY, Sissie did not believe in throwing anything away. Only by force was she willing to part with a broken dish or a warped picture frame. "Who knows, I might need all this junk one day," was her reasoning.

During the time she and Butch lived next door to Mother, Sissie collected everything that pleased her fancy, but when that house became overloaded with treasures and business was on the upswing, they bought a long, low ranch-style house just inside the Woodville city limits. "It'll take her a long time to fill this one up," everyone said. But it didn't take Sissie any time at all. Before long the house was packed to the rafters with grandfather clocks and artificial flowers, old cedar chests, rifles, fishing gear, broken down bedsteads, more tables and chairs than a family would ever need, and God only knows how many knickknack shelves overflowing with whatnots. Shag rugs our grandmother had made from nylons were strewn throughout the house, and Christmas decorations fell out of every closet along with old clothes, hats, shoes, sweaters, and sewing machines. In every room family photographs and religious prints papered the walls, and wherever you sat there was no wanting for cookie jars, vases, aquariums, bird cages, lamps of all sizes, and crocks filled with walking sticks. Everything was neatly arranged, meticulously so. There was even a pool table, a Wurlitzer juke box, a foosball table, and a large electric fan that never left the master bedroom.

No matter how cold the winters may be, Sissie cannot sleep without an electric fan blowing directly on her. In the summer she air-conditions the bedroom to such an extremely low temperature that she requires an electric blanket as well as a fan going full blast. She's always been this way, so there's no need to worry about her at this point, nor Butch either. He has adjusted beautifully.

Fortunately for Sissie, the ranch house had two garages, because soon after moving in she bought an extra car, a 1965 black Cadillac in need of serious repair; in fact it wouldn't even start. She parked the Cadillac in the spare garage and used the front and back seats as well as the trunk to store broken toys, kitchen gadgets, encyclopedias, *National Geographic* magazines, overcoats, and anything else she needed to get out of the house.

Sissie purchased the Cadillac from her brother-in-law, who had purchased it from his boss, who said that he had placed the winning bid at the Movie World Auction Company in Hollywood, California. Sissie paid one thousand dollars in cash for the limousine and considered that a steal because its former owner had been John Wayne.

Stuffed with castoffs and collectibles from floor to ceiling, John Wayne's Cadillac sat in the garage for several years. Occasionally, someone would ask to come see it and Sissie would say: "All right, I'll show it to you but only if you promise me you won't open the doors, we'll never get them closed again if you do."

She figured if she kept the car long enough it would be worth something even though she had no papers proving former ownership. But alas, during hard times, the Cadillac didn't bring in a dime; the ranch style home did. It sold to the Church of Christ to be used as a parsonage for a new preacher who had already started moving himself into town. For the time being he was storing his possessions in the former parsonage, a modest frame house that Sissie and Butch bought from the church, even though it meant cutting their living space in half.

Unfortunately, the lot on which the former parsonage sat was not for sale, so my cousins agreed to move the house themselves. Meanwhile, the incoming preacher was filling it up with his own belongings. Sissie stood in her yard and watched him with grave concern. "If he fills that house up with his own things we'll never get moved in," she said. "He should wait until I figure out what to do with all my stuff. Then I'll move in over there and he can move in over here."

But nothing would slow the man down. Every day he arrived with another load of furnishings, and finally, Sissie took things into her own hands. The second he left town to make another haul, she called the house movers, and when the preacher returned later that day there was no parsonage at the end of the driveway. Not only that, during the move, lamps were broken, furniture was scratched, and a pedigreed cat got loose and could not be found. "He shouldn't have left his fancy cat in there all by itself," Sissie said. Suddenly, there was talk of a lawsuit, but nothing ever came of it, and for a long time, no one was very happy except my cousin. She had solved her problem. With the help of two United Portable buildings placed in her new back yard, she was able to move from eight rooms into four rooms without getting rid of anything, including John Wayne's Cadillac. She parked it under a shed in a friend's backyard, and there it sits to this very day.

Not too long ago, I was back in Woodville searching high and low for the photograph of Aunt Horty in her coffin. "Go look in John Wayne's Cadillac," Sissie said, "but be careful. It's full of snakes and everything else."

She was right. And if Aunt Horty's photograph is there, there it will stay guarded by snakes, spiders, and firecrackers.

Sissie believes in having plenty of firecrackers scattered

throughout her house as well as the outdoor storage buildings. In every box and bureau drawer, in every closet and hamper there are firecrackers of all sizes. Some are loose, but most are still in their packages. "Just in case the house catches fire in the middle of the night," Sissie said. "I'll be the first to know about it. I'll at least be able to save *some* of my things."

During my last visit something unexpected came over Sissie. Suddenly she decided she wanted to clean out her United Portable buildings and throw everything away. I volunteered to help, and in spite of the ninety-degree temperature and high humidity we threw away over two hundred industrial-strength garbage bags filled with moth-eaten clothes, fishing tackle, odd lengths of rope, sacks of empty Polygrip bottles, and I don't know what all else. No one could believe she was, at last, parting with all her things, and when the United Portable sheds were almost empty, she stood in the largest one and sighed with relief: "Eddie Jr., I believe I could live out here, and I just might. All I would need is a bed and my fan."

"But what about Butch?"

"He'd get along," she replied. "He don't need an electric fan the way I do."

IN THE TWO WEEKS it took us to clean out those two sheds we ate one watermelon a day to give us strength to go on and something to look forward to. Because of the heat we took frequent sit-downs on the side porch. In fact, we started our days there.

Every morning I got up early and sat on the porch swing to read. Before long, Sissie would appear in her sleeping costume, pink cotton pants and a long white smock with large blue buttons like something a commedia dell'arte character might wear. While

Woodville was waking up, we would talk about this and that, and one morning she told me about her friend Old Tom. He too was a collector, and because of that Sissie sympathized with him over his latest predicament.

Tom lived near a large lake estate where retirees have settled, but he wasn't much of a homebody. Somewhere back in the Thicket he built himself a deer stand, a small one-room house on stilts with tiny windows for shooting. There he spent most of his time, whether it was deer hunting season or not, and no one could imagine what had possessed him to take up residence in a deer stand where there was hardly enough room to turn around. Then one day a strong wind blew the deer stand down, and Tom's collection of ladies' underwear went flying all over the woods. It seems he had been breaking into various houses in the area just to steal panties and brassieres from wives, all of whom he knew.

"What did he want with all those panties and brassieres?" Sissie wondered. "Try them on, I guess. It's the only thing I can think of."

When Old Tom was caught red-handed with the goods every-one teased him unmercifully. They said he would go to jail for stealing if the law ever found out. The thought of being locked up preyed upon his mind, and after sleepless nights he decided to give back everything he had stolen. Going door to door, he made an attempt to return every last panty and bra to its rightful owner, but of course, everyone turned him away. He even called Clinton on the telephone: "Clint," he said, "I have a few things that belong to your lady, and I sure would like to give them back." Clinton cussed him for every goddamn son of a bitching thing he could lay tongue on, and not long after that Old Tom decided to move to a nearby town and lay low for awhile.

"Eddie Jr.," Sissie said, after she had told me this story, "I know how awful it can be to collect things. After you get started you just can't stop to save your life, but if Old Tom had only come to me, I'd have given him all the underwear he wanted. Maybe that would have kept him out of trouble."

While she told me this story she was tweezing her chin whiskers, a ritual she performs each morning without fail. Still in her sleeping costume, she hurries to catch the early light. Then she balances a hand mirror and a cup of coffee on the porch rail and tweezes away.

One morning when she was involved with this little task she declaimed, "Eddie Jr., I have never seen the like of chin whiskers on any one woman before in my life. I believe I'm about to turn into a man for sure."

"Sissie," I said, "all of Woodville can drive by and see you out here tweezing your whiskers." To this my cousin replied:

"Who gives a rat's ass about Woodville at a time like this?"

Woodville

T HE TYLER COUNTY courthouse in Woodville is a stucco building of three square tiers stacked one on top of the other like a wedding cake without decorations. Underneath the stucco is a Texas Gothic courthouse, a beautiful building hidden behind a mask of plaster, sharp corners, and hard edges. From the very beginning, I saw the courthouse as a metaphor. Even before I knew what a metaphor was, I knew the courthouse was one. I don't know how I knew. I just did. Perhaps Grandmother, the great reader in the family, understood this too and somehow passed it on.

Growing up in the shadow of such a building, and with Grandfather's finger looming behind a stack of bath towels, my cousins and I were practically forced to develop imagination and curiosity, to turn our thoughts inward, and to ask questions, the kind that have no easy answers. As for me, I became a novelist. The Tyler County courthouse and Grandfather's finger helped point me in this direction—for better or for worse.

To this day I cannot walk through Woodville without stopping to face our courthouse. It is nothing more than a mask, and yet, it is so obviously a mask that it deserves some attention, if not respect. The courthouse is, as I have written in another book, like someone who is hiding something that he has no business hiding but has been made to feel like he has business hiding it so he does. The courthouse is like someone in disguise, someone who is ashamed of what he looks like so he's allowed everyone else to make him over to look like what they wanted him to look like whether he wants it or not. Underneath the shield there is a proud, old building.

Years ago, the elected county officials and everyone else who worked in the courthouse were given, upon retirement, a photograph of the original building, the one covered up. That was the Woodville we moved into.

Towns and institutions that conceal themselves behind layers of plaster and protocol seem to produce an extremely variegated assortment of humanity. I am told it's the same everywhere, but I am not so sure about that. I do know this: in places where there are so many rules to be broken and masks to be worn, there are always people who are willing to break loose out of frustration and sheer amusement. They are the ones who make us smile or roll our eyes. They entertain us. And Woodville has always had more than its share of entertainers. It has also had its share of lynching, robbery, drug addiction, and murder.

Not long after we arrived, I was sitting at the drugstore soda fountain while murder was being committed in the bus station only a few steps away. The bus station and the drugstore were in different rooms of the same building but connected by double doors that were kept open. From the soda fountain I could see into the waiting room but could not see who was waiting for the three o'clock bus—a mother holding her infant. The baby was crying unmercifully, and the noise was putting the soda jerk's nerves on edge. Her name was Marie, and she kept saying to me:

Woodville courthouse, before and after renovation

"If that baby doesn't stop crying, I'm going to go in there and cut its head off. So help me I am."

A few minutes later, the baby suddenly stopped crying. "Thank God," Marie said. "Now I won't have to break the law."

When the bus arrived the mother boarded it with only a suitcase in her hands. No child could be seen. Poor Marie was the first to spot a bloody rag hanging out of the suitcase. One might have expected her to fall apart, but she didn't. She didn't even register the slightest emotion. Without neglecting her customers, she merely picked up the telephone and called the police. Then the bus departed. And in the next town the suitcase was opened. The baby was dead, strangled with shoelaces, and the mother's only explanation was:

"It was driving me crazy."

"Perfectly understandable," my grandmother said.

The murderess pleaded temporary insanity and was sentenced to a very short term in prison.

"Temporary insanity can happen to anyone," Grandmother announced. "Particularly around here."

MOVING TO WOODVILLE was very hard on everyone except Eva Gay. At last, she was in her element, but the rest of us were not so fast to adjust, and the trauma of moving twice in one year may have been the final straw in Grandfather's life; it was just more than he could endure. Coming from Camp Ruby, Woodville, population 1,700, looked like a big city to us. At first the place was intimidating. "Townspeople are not like country people." I heard my relatives say this. "They have high and mighty ways about them."

I soon found out for myself that they could be extremely judgmental. When I wore my green dancing skirt into town, everyone looked askance. They clicked their tongues. I couldn't imagine why. When I demonstrated my skill *en pointe* their faces registered alarm. Fortunately, we never lived inside the town limits, and therefore I retained a certain distance from those mean streets, but only until I adjusted to them.

In school it was just the same, only worse. Trying to make conversation with my peers was a nightmare. Grandfather's finger, apricot pits, and dead frogs in the bottom of Coke bottles did little to convince anyone that I was a normal human being. When I opened my mouth most of the pupils ran the other way because I had nothing to talk about except Aunt Coleta's diatribes on gypsies, the grave of the Mexican baby, and Grandfather urinating on the Christmas tree. I had nothing to talk about except uncles boiled in oil, atomic bombs, bloody bones, the Mark of the Beasts, and wildcats that screamed like headless women. Didn't everyone know that the Devil in disguise watches us from the top of the tallest tree? *No!* I was told. Didn't everyone know that a red-headed Jesus lived somewhere beyond the stove pipe hole in our Camp Ruby ceiling? *Certainly not!* I was quickly informed.

Who could imagine going to public school and talking about such things? I made a few very close friends in every grade, but by and large I and my pals were certifiable by local standards.

Sissie and Clinton were far more socially accepted. They had the good sense to keep their mouths shut. I did not. Never have. But they also had the splendid fortune of being sent to a school located in the far reaches of the Big Thicket. Big Sandy, it was called. It was a country school, a good one, and they were well adjusted. I was a mess.

Early on in elementary school, I recall mentioning the Big

Thicket and listening to the teachers and students laugh. "Woodville is certainly not the Big Thicket," I was told. "Woodville is a town. The Big Thicket exists somewhere else, over near Saratoga, maybe. Over near Sour Lake, maybe. Somewhere over there, *way* over there." I knew immediately that I was not where I wanted to be. I was terrified of everyone: teachers, peers, janitors, the ladies behind the cafeteria line. Everyone looked mean. I preferred the adults in my family. They talked, and I listened without having to respond. I enjoyed that. But school was not for me. Reciting made me nervous. Recess made me nervous. Older students made me nervous. Younger students made me nervous. And the teachers made me nervous and angry at the same time. Every year at least one teacher took me aside and said, "Can't you try to fit in? Can't you try to be like everyone else? People want to be able to like you, but they don't know how. People want to know who you are."

Little did they know, I didn't have a chance in hell of being like the others, and for that matter, neither did many of my cousins, although some of them have practically killed themselves trying to fit in. Fortunately, I knew I was a hopeless case, and my only recourse was to make the best of it until I could find my own place.

My grandmother did very little to make it easier on me. Thanks to her I went to school with a rarefied vocabulary, most of which has been lost over the years. "Do you always talk like that?" I was asked. "Where do you get those silly words?" At some point I became so intimidated I edited all of Grandmother's words right out of my brain, and today I would pay a lot of money to have them put back in. Surely, I keep telling myself, they are still up there somewhere.

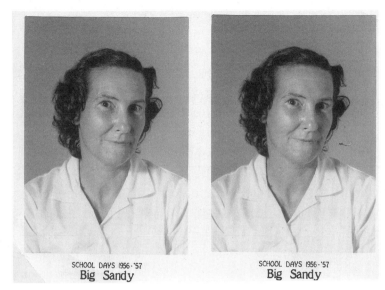

SCHOOL DAYS 1956-'57
Big Sandy

SCHOOL DAYS 1956-'57
Big Sandy

Aunt Coleta when she worked in the cafeteria at Big Sandy School

Words were always a problem. I seemed to know more than I needed to know, but not the ones that everyone else knew. One year during Halloween one of the older boys wrote "fuck you" all over the sidewalks. I was in the fourth grade. "What does 'fuck' mean?" I asked everyone. All the students laughed, and the teachers hushed me, but no one, not even Grandmother, the wordsmith, would attempt a definition.

Finally, Sissie and Grandmother decided they would teach me the facts of life, a lesson I shall never forget. It happened shortly after Frank's incarceration. Mother, along with other members of the family, had traveled to Arkansas to attend Frank's trial, leaving Grandmother and her broken bones at home with Sissie and me. We were supposed to take care of her, to make sure she ate properly, and to give her shots of insulin. It was my job to administer the shots, a task I greatly enjoyed because every time I plunged the needle into Grandmother's arm or leg she jumped as if mortally wounded.

One evening we were sitting up late, just the three of us, when Grandmother, speaking as if I were not in the room, said to Sissie, "Eddie Jr. doesn't know the *facts,* and Pearl can't find the sense it takes to tell him anything, so let's teach him a few things as we go along."

In an irritating, all too grown up voice, Sissie (no more than six years my senior) replied—as if I were not present—"Grandmother, Eddie Jr. sure does need to know about *life."*

Then Grandmother turned to me with an expression of mock surprise, as if she had just discovered that I was sitting only inches away. With her tiny, sharp eyes glued to mine, she said, "What you don't understand is that it takes a hen and a rooster to make a chick."

Then Sissie, speaking in a sanctimonious tone, added, "And it takes a cow and a bull to make a little calf."

This is all I was told. The extent of it. But when everyone came back from Arkansas an announcement was made: "Eddie Jr. knows about *life* now."

I wanted to run away and never come back.

Finally, I convinced myself that I had only three weeks to live. Relief was in sight! I would never again endure a moment's worth of humiliation, neither by Grandmother and Sissie nor by the students at school. "It will almost be over," I kept assuring myself. The three weeks stretched into four, five into six, and still I continued believing that my time was running out. Somehow I managed to live long enough to join the junior high school band. I chose to play the flute because it was held sideways. That appealed to my sense of life as being something off center. Very soon the music students became my closest friends. We practiced constantly to the neglect of our other subjects and were often taking trips and entering contests. We won medals and trophies for solos and ensembles, for marching in formation, for concert playing, for baton-twirling, and who knows what else. Suddenly, and for the first time since leaving Camp Ruby, life was grand again.

About that time I went to work at the Fain Theater, our local movie house. Mr. Wood Fain gave me a job selling popcorn for a dollar a night. I was in seventh grade and thought I had struck it rich. For a little more than a year, I saw every film that came to town, but today I only remember a few: *The King and I, An American in Paris, Roman Holiday, Baby Doll,* and *Broken Arrow* with Jeff Chandler. Then there was some Sophia Loren disaster about dolphins and quite a few Randolph Scott westerns. I don't remember the westerns, but I do remember *him.* He wore his six shooters slung so low I could not help wondering what was holding them up. Randolph Scott made an indelible impression on me, but so did Debra Paget, especially when she was forced to jump into an active volcano to appease the gods. The movie may have been *Bird of Paradise,* and the actress may have been Rosanna Podesta, not Debra Paget. I could find out for sure by asking my cousin Ben, who married Debra Paget's sister, but why go to all the trouble only to discover it was another movie or another actress?

All in all, I could not have asked for a better first job. My coworker liked it too. He tore tickets and changed the marquee. I handed him the letters and held the ladder steady. His name was Chris.

Chris was the son of a preacher, a country preacher, I suppose you could say, as opposed to a town preacher. His father was not sanctimonious, was not quick to judge, and there was nothing fancy about him. He was of the earth. He preached in small, out-of-the-way chapels back in the woods. He was likable and had beautiful manners, and so did his wife. Their son became my best friend.

Every Saturday morning Chris and I met at the theater to clean it up a bit. He swept out the auditorium, and I scoured the popcorn machine. We worked rapidly because other things were on our minds. We had plans and were eager to get on with them. After finishing our duties we hurried to the back of the theater and climbed a wobbly ladder to the second-story roof. There we picked chinaberries off the trees and tested our slingshots. Only when we were fully armed and our weapons in good working order did we advance to the front of the building. There, crouching behind the parapet, we surveyed the street through drainage holes and waited for a Saturday crowd to gather on the courthouse square. Very soon, full-figured matrons, whose dignity had not yet been violated, strolled innocently into target range, and instantly we opened fire with chinaberry ammunition, nipping them on their tender breasts or behinds. We always set our sights on ladies of impressive girth, not because they made easier targets but because they were vociferous and fast to react. They screamed or swooned loudly. They clutched their bosoms, rubbed their thighs, and waddled down the street under a storm of chinaberries.

One Saturday afternoon an irate wife who had just been battered and bruised in delicate places heard us laughing on the roof. "Up there they are!" she shouted and dispatched her husband to fetch us down. Reluctantly, he came around to the back of the theater and tried to climb the ladder. Half way up his knees began shaking. Vertigo got the better of him, and finally he eased his way down and left us alone. We were thankful for that.

Thereafter, we gave up our slingshots for somewhat safer pastimes. After rushing through our Saturday chores we would sometimes catch a ride to Chris's house, about two miles outside the town limits. There we would swim in a muddy pond and try to think of something to amuse ourselves. Somehow, we hit upon the idea of picking fleas off one of Chris's dogs and putting them in an aspirin bottle. Then we carried the bottled fleas to the Fain Theater, and when Adell Brown, the lady who sold tickets, turned her back on us, we surreptitiously emptied the bottle of fleas on her head and shoulders.

Adell was my mother's first cousin by marriage. All dolled up she sat in her glassed-in booth and sold tickets while gossiping on the telephone. In the back of the booth was a narrow door that opened into the lobby of the theater, and when we heard Adell's voice rise with excitement we took it as our cue to deposit the fleas and make a fast getaway.

How many times did we pull this trick? Dozens and dozens I'm sure. And did we ever tire of it? Certainly not! Sometimes Adell would wear a dress that was cut low in the back, and then we had the great pleasure of depositing the fleas directly on her fair skin. That was always a thrilling moment. Seeing those fleas hopping around on her bare flesh brought us to the edge of hysterics, but seeing the red whelps on her back carried us completely out of control. All we did was laugh. And not once did Adell catch on. She was always complaining about mosquitoes and spraying her ticket booth. For at least a year she reeked of insect repellent.

But we didn't stop there.

One Saturday afternoon when Chris came home with me, we decided to wrap up an empty box as if it were a Christmas present and leave it alongside the highway just to see if anyone would stop and pick it up. Sure enough someone did. After that we wrapped up another box with beautiful paper and colorful ribbons. This time we tied a string onto it, and when a motorist came to a screeching halt, we pulled the box into the bushes and watched the puzzled driver searching for something he was quite sure he had seen but was no longer there. This has to be one of the oldest tricks in the world, and we certainly made good use of it. As we went along, our boxes became larger and more elaborately wrapped, making it difficult to pull them into the bushes in a hurry. One Saturday afternoon an angry driver chased us far into the woods. We escaped. But that brought an end to the oldest trick in the world.

By then we were losing our inspiration fast, and our interests were not developing along the same lines. We both quit our jobs at about the same time. I don't remember what reasons we gave, but suddenly I understood that nothing was the same, nor would it ever be the same again. In other words, Chris grew up, and I did not. He put away childish pursuits, but I refused. Overnight, or so it seemed, he became more interested in girls than in me, and I, desperate for a new playmate, turned my attention to a newcomer, a bouncy youth director employed by the First Baptist Church.

Her name was Betty Jones. She came from Louisiana, graduated from a seminary in New Orleans, and was considered *fast* by local standards. I do not mean to imply that she was sexually active. No indeed. In fact, she was probably a virgin. But she had ways that were different, and therefore she was *suspect*. As Director of Youth Activities, she was often criticized for fraternizing with the young people, particularly the boys.

I liked her because she had studied drama. She could sing Broadway songs and talk about a man named Tennessee Williams. Unlike the other Baptists, Betty believed in dancing, smoking, and moderate drinking. She was always mentioning Tom Collins as if talking about a favorite beau, and for the longest time I thought she was.

She also loved movies as much as I.

One night after prayer meeting the two of us left the Baptist church and walked half a block to the Fain Theater, where the Brigitte Bardot classic *And God Created Woman* was being shown. There was a much talked about nude scene in the film, harmless by today's standards, and we were anxious to see Bardot stripped bare. I was a freshman in high school, and we were the only two people in the audience for the second showing. At the time, I remember thinking, *we're going to get into a lot of trouble over this.*

The next day all of Woodville was buzzing with talk about the Baptist youth director who was out to corrupt as many young people as she could lay hands on. "She's become too close with that Eddie Swift," it was said. "So what?" Mother argued. Within a week Betty Jones was fired. Gone. Run out of town in less than a year. And from then on the Baptist Church kept a close eye on the films that were being shown and who attended them. Fingers were pointed every time someone stepped out of line. For after all, God was watching. And so the masks went up, and the parade continued, and those who stood on the curb and refused to march were dismissed.

I CRIED and cried when Betty Jones was run out of town, but very soon I fixed on another playmate, a skinny baton twirler named Linda Margaret. She twirled her baton aggressively, flinging it around as if it were a weapon. I felt safe in her presence, and by then I desperately needed some protection because I was being picked on left and right by every football player in school, especially Bull Poindexter.

"I'm gonna catch you after school," he would say, pressing a finger into my facial birthmark, "and when I do I'm gonna put another scar on that face of yours." I was scared to death of Bull Poindexter, and when I saw him coming I would look for Kathleen Mahan or Linda Margaret or any other girl with a baton in hand and the courage to stand up to a brute.

Baton twirlers were my friends, and I felt especially close to Linda Margaret. But it was not love. No indeed, for already I knew in my heart, if not my head, that my membership belonged in an entirely different church. I'm quite sure that she knew it too. She was no fool. And I was crazy about her.

She called me *Swift*. I called her *Margo*. And we called our group of intimates the *Comrades*. Margo thought of the name, and naturally, we went along with her. There were five of us if my memory serves me: Kathleen Mahan, a flute-playing baton twirler whose father worked at the bank and played the organ at the Baptist church; John Reid, a trumpet player who lived in town not far from Margo; and John's sister, Linda, who eventually gained respectability by becoming a Dogwood Queen. We were the Comrades, and we wanted everyone to know it. Our ringleader was Margo, and we trusted her implicitly. She pointed the way, and we followed without question.

Several times she sneaked us into the Rainy Hotel, a two-story frame building with galleries on both levels. Pretending to be invisible, she led us through the front door and up the central staircase, and if not that, she had us climbing a sycamore and stepping from the branches onto an upper gallery in order to enter the hotel through a screen door that was never latched. From there we tiptoed single file down a long hallway to a closet. Inside it there was a hidden stairway that Margo had discovered on one of her solo adventures. She took pleasure in leading us up this dusty staircase and into the dark, hot attic where there was a large quilt box about as long as a bathtub. Margo told us that there was a dead man inside the box, and she dared us to open it and have a look. Of course, no one was brave enough to do such a thing, no one except Margo. She sometimes tortured us by slowly opening the lid only an inch or two. The hinges squeaked ominously and so did her voice. "Now you're going to see the dead man," she would say. "You better get ready." Suddenly she would throw open the lid and close it just as fast giving us little time to catch a glimpse of anything. "Now you've seen it," she'd whisper. "Now you've seen the dead man." The rest of us would break out in a cold sweat. Margo could make us believe almost anything.

For Halloween, or school carnivals, or any social event, the Comrades, led by the baton-twirling Margo, terrorized the festivities. Once we baked persimmons until they were mushy and splattered them on our enemies. But that wasn't good enough, and soon we fixed our sights on more serious ammunition. Armed with a shovel and disposable pie pans, Margo led us to a cow pasture to collect fresh manure. We packed the manure into the pie pans and decorated the tops with shaving cream. Those fresh manure pies became our trademark. They were our most dreaded weapon, and we hurled them at any unfortunate peer who happened to cross our path. Before long we were being challenged by other teams of kids, but we were never caught off guard. Thanks to Margo we managed to have ammunition at our fingertips. Lord only knows how many cow manure pies landed on Ronnie Warfield's head and shoulders. He was a polite, good-natured boy with keen intelligence, and he deserved better treatment than what we gave him. But why apologize now?

We thought we were daring, the five of us. We thought we were clever, and we were very proud of ourselves. We were hellions, or liked to think we were. But this little phase of close friendship soon faded into other activities. Margo, who played bassoon, became seriously interested in becoming one of the six majorettes in the high school marching band. From then on she religiously practiced the fundamentals of baton twirling until she could catch aerials behind her back, until her finger spins, two-hand spins, and horizontals were absolutely perfect. And of course, she made the grade.

While the Comrades were in full swing, my interest in music

diminished more than slightly, but when Margo turned with un-mitigated vengeance toward serious baton twirling, I, needing something to occupy my restlessness, returned to my flute play-ing with diligence to spare. For hours on end I practiced my scales and with such dreadful seriousness as to almost convince myself that I was appointed by God to be the instrument's next interpreter. I made all-region band four years in a row, but only because I spent all my time with a flute, and later on, a piccolo in my hands. I even developed the uncompromising skill of driving Mother's car with my knees while practicing my scales in two octaves. And why was I never arrested for this? There can only be one reason: by then, no one, not even the Texas Highway Pa-trol, wanted to get Mother riled up.

Although I started out with the flute and had a slight talent for the instrument, the piccolo appealed to me the most. Somehow it was more to the point, and Bull Poindexter thought so too. "What do you do with that piccolo when you go to bed at night?" he would ask me, especially if lots of students were listening. I endured his dreaded presence with feigned dignity, but it wasn't easy. At the age of fifteen, it was humiliating. Today, I could give many impressive answers to Bull Poindexter's indelicate question, but back then everything was tender. Everything hurt. Every-thing was embarrassing. So I practiced my flute, memorized John Philip Sousa on the piccolo, and *marched on.*

We had a good marching band and some very fine, naturally gifted musicians. Sadly, I wasn't really one of them. My flute play-ing was just above average, and my piccolo was always too sharp, my vibrato completely out of control. "Too shrill," everyone said. "Pipe down." But I had a very poor ear and could hardly deter-mine sharp from flat, and besides that, what did I care? As long as I could be heard in the obbligato section of *Stars and Stripes Forever*, nothing else mattered, not until my fascination turned toward Ouija boards, crystal balls, and fortune telling.

No doubt Great-Aunt Rachel Durham had something to do with my inclination toward the mysterious. She was a water witch. On the porch of her dog-run house hung a dowsing rod, a willow branch shaped like a capital Y with a long tail. When asked to find the best place to dig a water well, Aunt Rachel would hold the rod by each fork and walk with the stem pointed straight out. If there was water underground, the branch would point downward as if it had a mind of its own. At times it reacted violently, almost leaping out of Aunt Rachel's hands. "Sink your shovels here!" she would say to the well diggers. "This is where you'll find water and plenty of it." They say she was never wrong.

To my disappointment, when I held Aunt Rachel's dowsing rod nothing happened at all. The willow branch did not even wobble in my hands, but when consulting Mrs. Lynn Williams's magic card table answers were received. Although they may not have been the answers any of us wanted, at least the table responded.

Margo's mother, Mrs. Lynn Williams, had a very old, well-worn card table, and with a few magic words and three devout believers she could make it *talk*. First we decided what questions we wanted to ask. Then we lightly placed the palms of our hands on the table. With thumbs touching thumbs and little fingers touching little fingers we formed an unbroken circle. "Whatever you do," Mrs. Williams would remind us several times an evening, "don't break our connection, not even if you have to stand up or scratch your nose. If you do the spirits won't talk to us tonight."

With our hands correctly placed, she would wait for a moment of complete silence. Then she would say:

"If the spirits are willing and the table is full charged, please rise to the medium please rise."

After everyone had repeated this chant individually Mrs. Williams would continue, "Table, if I am a medium, bow over to me." The table would then tip over on two legs and Mrs. Williams would say, "Thank you, Table. Table, will you talk to us tonight? Rap once for yes and twice for no."

If, indeed, the spirits were willing and the table fully charged, it would lean toward Mrs. Williams and rap once for yes. Then she would proceed by asking the table one of our questions, and if it could not be answered *yes* or *no,* she would instruct the table to spell out the answer, one rap for the letter A, two raps for the letter B, three raps for the letter C, and so on and so forth. When the spirits were talkative, a seance could last quite a long time, and we would stay to the bitter end.

Quite often Mrs. Williams would ask, "Table, is there another medium here tonight? If there is, rap once for yes and twice for no." If the table answered *yes,* each person would be given an opportunity to address the spirits by saying, "Table, if I am a medium, bow over to me." If the table chose a new medium that person would take charge by asking questions until the spirits stopped talking or the table bowed to another leader.

Toward the end of a seance, the raps were sometimes very feeble, as if the spirits were running out of energy. To bring an evening to a close, Mrs. Williams would say, "Table, are you through talking to us tonight?" The table usually answered *yes* or ignored the question entirely. "The spirits are tired now," Mrs. Williams would announce. "We'd better stop."

Once after a Sunday evening church service, Margo and I, along with two other friends, attempted to conduct a seance in

Fellowship Hall. We were using a fairly new card table found in a closet and were not having much luck, so Mrs. Williams sat down to assist. Several prominent Baptists barged in on us and raised hell. "Seances are the work of the Devil," we were told. "Seances are not to be held in or near God's house." Thereafter, we were never allowed to work our magic in the church, but that didn't stop us from talking to the spirits in Mrs. Williams's living room.

After church services on Sunday night we would say, "Oh, Mrs. Williams, do you think the spirits will talk to us tonight?"

"Let's go find out," she would say. "But don't let anyone know."

The Samarian Woman

L IKE MY GRANDFATHER, the only thing I enjoyed about church was the singing. In Camp Ruby hymns were sung with energy. Sometimes they were practically shouted with joy. But in the First Baptist Church of Woodville the same hymns were sung in a restrained manner. Suddenly they seemed ordinary. No one broke loose with spirit. People stuck to the hymn books and to what was written. They followed the rules. Then one Sunday I heard a new voice, a high piercing soprano that could be heard above all the others. The singer was a round, red-haired lady in her mid-forties, and her name was Louise Owens. She and her husband had just moved to town. He was quiet. She was talkative. And before long people were saying that she should learn to control her tongue, that she was too flamboyant, too spirited. They also said that she should be locked up, that she was downright crazy.

But Louise Owens, like Hardy Cain, lacked a lot being crazy.

LOUISE called herself a devout child of God with a song in her heart. "I have a new message to give an old world," she preached, "and I have a way of delivering it that will make people sit up and listen." Her husband was an ordained Baptist minister serving as regional missionary, and he made it quite clear that he did not agree with his wife's unorthodox practices. "We don't have a thing in common," she often said. "He doesn't understand me, and my children don't understand me either. Nobody understands me anymore, nobody but Jesus."

I don't know if her husband understood her or not, but I do know that he was alarmed by her theatrics.

Louise said that drama started in the church and should be returned to the church, immediately if not sooner. To achieve this, she wrote an inspirational monologue entitled *The Samarian Woman,* and she traveled in full costume and makeup all over the Big Thicket delivering this highly theatrical presentation to congregations so remote it was a mystery how she ever found them. Often she enlisted me to go along and deliver an introduction. I was in high school and had nothing better to do for entertainment, so I usually agreed. She told me what to say, and I stood before the congregations and delivered her words as if they were my own:

"Louise Owens is an inspired child of God, a talented songwriter, singer, and preacher, as well as a dramatic actress, who has dedicated her talent for the ongoing of God's word . . ."

Her costume for these occasions was an old white wedding dress with a voluminous skirt and a long veil that she coiled around one arm when walking. Why she thought this was appropriate dress for a Samarian woman, I will never know, but her Samarian costume never changed and neither did her makeup. For these intimate gatherings of backwoods Christians, Louise painted her face as if she were a diva. She also decorated herself with an enormous quantity of necklaces, rings, and bracelets, along with several brooches, one of which she invariably wore on her head.

On the evenings of her performances she would pick me up in her Volkswagen and away we would go, she in her Samarian outfit, I in my black suit with yards and yards of wedding skirt spilling onto my lap, billowing out the windows, and obscuring vision through the windshield. Along the way we would sing her theme song, "Oh! the Holy Ghost Will Set Your Feet A-dancing." And, after tiring of that, we would move on to her second all-time favorite:

He's coming. He's coming. He's coming. He's coming.
He's coming. He's coming.
Today.

The second verse is just the same, only different:

He loves me. He loves me. He loves me. He loves me.
He loves me. He loves me.
I know.

Louise wrote dozens of verses to this deceivingly simple little song, and we managed to sing all of them in full voice before arriving at our faraway destinations. Traveling through river bottoms and across dirt roads that disappeared into the underbrush was no problem for her. Fate was on her side, and a prayer was in her heart. All along the way she pleaded to Jesus to guide our every twist and turn. "Don't let the Devil lead us astray," she would shout. "Get thee behind me, Satan, for I am about to deliver the word of God in a new and exciting way to people who are ready to receive it."

If the roads were wet and the mud holes bottomless, she would beg me to pray for a safe journey. "Darling!" she would exclaim. "Pray to Jesus that we don't get stuck. Lost souls are depending on us tonight." Then I, for no other reason but to appease her, would bow my head and say, "Lord Jesus, whatever you do, please don't let us get stuck." That usually pacified her for awhile.

We never did get stuck going to a performance, but I often wondered just what would have happened if we had. I held visions of Louise in her wedding dress, veil, and costume jewelry pushing the Volkswagen out of the mud, but that, I knew perfectly well, she would never have done. Had we gotten stuck, she would have more than likely turned to prayer. She believed deeply in praying for miracles and good samaritans. "Somebody always comes along in a time of need," she said. "God never abandons His children, even when it seems like He has. When you think He's left you what He's really doing is testing your faith." With mixed tones of pride and resentment, she would sometimes add, "He has certainly tested mine to the fullest. He has given me a husband who doesn't understand my heart, and I am persuaded to love him in spite of it."

Because the churches we visited were extremely remote and the directions for finding them never specific, we usually arrived late. The congregations would be standing around waiting for us, and Louise, blowing the horn to signal her arrival, would stop and throw open the door. Her enormous skirt would billow out of the car like a cloud, and soon she would follow it.

Frequently, we visited churches that were so isolated the people in the area never went into town except once or twice a year. When *they* saw Louise getting out of the car, they often ran the other way. Never had they seen anything quite like her. I don't think it was the jewels and dress they found so startling but her elaborate eye makeup and her bright cheeks, lips, and golden-red hair. At times, she appeared to be possessed, and her high-pitched voice did little to persuade people otherwise. To an

Big Thicket Church

impatient congregation waiting for her outside a church she would speak as if singing descant: "I have come to deliver the word of God as it has been handed down though Jesus Christ to the Samarian Woman and finally to me. Eddie Swift will make an introduction just as soon as everyone goes inside and sits down."

After my introduction, Louise strolled down the aisle as if in a heavenly trance, and who knows, perhaps she was. Her veil swept the floor clean, and if there were hymnals, Sunday school magazines, or collection plates lying on tables and pews, they were often knocked to the floor by the movement of her astonishing skirt. At the altar she would face the congregation with her eyes closed, and when the Lord led her she would open them abruptly. Without fail, the churchgoers would gasp and squirm. "I am the Samarian Woman," she would begin. "I met Jesus at the well. He loved me when no one else would love me. He cared for me when no one else would care for me, and He *touched* me in a way I can never forget."

I don't remember much beyond her opening sentences and am not too sure the monologue had ever been written down. She seemed to write and rewrite it as the spirit led her along. I do remember, however, that this little drama lasted well over an hour and detailed every waking moment of the Samarian woman's life as a harlot, a woman used and abused by men of the world only to be cast aside like a dirty garment that only Jesus would touch.

After her last word, Louise invited the lost souls sitting before her (and she was always certain there were many) to step forward and accept Christ publicly. Here she would choose one of the standard invitational hymns such as "Wherever He Leads I'll Go." She would pitch the hymn so high no one could possibly sing along with her, and on finishing the last verse all alone, she would either start over or choose another hymn, "Just As I Am," perhaps, which she would also pitch higher than anyone else could sing. She had great physical reserve and could sing one invitational hymn right after another without tiring. She would sing and sing until someone stepped forward and accepted Christ or rededicated his life to God's service. Only then would she stop singing and say good-night.

Within a year or two, she had performed in every remote church in the Big Thicket, but received no invitations to return. Suddenly, everyone was talking about her as if she were a lunatic, but this did not faze Louise. She merely turned her energy toward organizing her own kind of church. While still living with her husband, she rented a small house where services could be held, and in the beginning the new congregation consisted of only two other women, Tiny Hill, who was short and stout, and Mary Flowers, who was tall and willowy. Both spoke in the unknown tongue and encouraged Louise to pray for a special God-given language. Very soon the Pentecostal spirit descended upon her, and from that day forward she referred to herself as Sister Louise, signing her name "Sis. Lou" for short.

During her early stages of sisterhood, Louise, seized by creative forces, composed one inspirational song right after another. She and her spiritual sisters, Mary and Tiny, along with a few carefully chosen guests, would get together and sing throughout the night. Crazed by the love of God, Sister Flowers would clap her hands and dance on tiptoes while singing jubilantly or spouting her Pentecostal language. Sister Louise would play the piano forcefully, and Sister Tiny Hill would beat wildly on her tambourine. Sister Louise always said:

"The tambourine is the very hardest instrument in the world

to learn how to play, but Sister Tiny sure does know how to play it. You've got to have God on your side to play a tambourine. Not many people know that."

Soon the new church had many members. People drove from neighboring towns and cities to attend a service and feel alive again. On occasions a preacher of like mind was invited to deliver a few inspired words, but most of the time everyone congregated just to sing, slap the Holy Spirit on each other, and deliver personal testimonies.

One evening, Sister Tiny Hill, who was in her mid-fifties and had never been married, surprised everyone by giving a testimony in which she announced her engagement. Naturally, she was apprehensive with regard to the demands of cohabitation, but she felt that the Lord was leading her down the path of holy matrimony, and therefore she had no choice but to follow. The congregation gave its unanimous approval, and Sister Tiny set her wedding date. Still she was consumed with unspeakable anxiety.

"If I can just get through the first night," she told my mother. "I think I'll be all right."

Mother said, "Tiny, it's not worth it. You're better off alone."

And to this Tiny replied, "Pearl, it's too late to back out."

The wedding came off without a hitch, but not the honeymoon. On her nuptial bed, Sister Tiny suffered a heart attack and was immediately hospitalized. With prayer on her lips, Sister Louise rushed to her friend's bedside, and while administering the laying on of hands, she prayed earnestly for a miracle. As it turned out, Sister Tiny made a remarkable recovery, and it may have been this very incident that convinced Louise Owens that she possessed the gift of healing. After Tiny's brush with death, Sister Louise slapped her healing hands on everyone in sight. "I don't

Sister Louise Owens and Tiny Hill

know if you're afflicted or not," she said to me one day in the post office, "but let me put my hands on your head just in case. If you're sick, God, working through me, will make you well."

Because Sister Louise's healing power was not exactly reliable, her friendship with Tiny Hill was destined to come to a rapid end. When it was learned that Tiny's husband was terminally ill, Louise announced, "I will heal him in the name of Jesus!" She had an attic bedroom, and in spite of Reverend Owen's protestations, she moved Sister Tiny and her husband into it. Several times a day and even in the middle of the night, Sister Louise climbed the narrow stairs to the attic. There she laid hands on Sister Tiny's husband and screamed, "Come out, sickness! Come out of this man's body." She prayed for his recovery. She sang for his recovery. She danced for his recovery. She did everything God led her to do, and within a few weeks Tiny's husband died in Louise's attic. Sister Tiny blamed Sister Louise. Sister Louise blamed Satan. Sister Flowers sided with Sister Louise, and Reverend Owens threatened to have his wife thrown in jail. Before long hardly anyone was speaking to the bereaved Tiny.

"What we need is a savior," Sister Louise announced. "Someone to pull us together and heal our wounds."

Shortly there appeared on the scene, and from God knows where, a Hindu who managed to convince Sister Louise that he was a disciple of Jesus Christ. To one and all, she confessed that this dark-eyed stranger had made a new woman out of her. "He's a saint," she testified. "He can bring sinners to their knees faster than anybody." Publicly, she counted her many blessings. "Thank you Lord," she exclaimed on every corner and avenue. "Thank you for putting this man in my life and giving me permission to love him." Then, staring deeply into the eyes of a listener, she would volunteer a few words of personal advice, "All you have to do is ask Him for permission to love and He will give it. He gave it to me, and He'll give it to you."

Before we knew it, Sister Louise and the preacher from India had disappeared. Most people believed they had run off together and were bedded up in some riverside motel, but others weren't so sure of that. According to rumor, he had been run out of town for romancing the local wives, and Louise had been committed to another asylum outside the state of Texas. Who can say what really happened? As far as I know, no one ever found out for sure, not even when Sister Louise reappeared as brightly dressed as ever and with eyes blazing with God's love renewed. She gave no explanation for her disappearance except to say, "The Holy Ghost knocked me flat on my face and I just had to lie there a while until I got over it." She said she had been slain by the Lord and that she would never be the same again.

The experience, it seemed, only slightly altered her point of view. Instead of *sealing* people in the name of Jesus she began *slaying* the sinners of the world. Slapping her victims on the forehead, she would shout, "I SLAY you in the name of Jesus of Nazareth." Everyone she slapped was supposed to fall backward, paralyzed by the power of God, but few, if any, did. Still she continued slapping foreheads right and left while shouting, "SLAY this sinner, Jesus."

Not too long after slaying half the population of Woodville, Sister Louise Owens disappeared yet again, and to this day she has not been seen in East Texas. No one seems to know exactly where she is, and unfortunately, no one seems to care.

Lila Williams, Pomp Meadows,
and the Secondhand Coffin

I F THEY DON'T LIKE YOU in Woodville, they'll get rid of you fast," said Lila Williams, Margo's great aunt. "If you don't believe me, just stick around and see." We were sitting on her porch. Lila was in her early seventies, and she claimed to know everything there was to know about Woodville. "I know who did the shooting and killing," she said. "I know who did the bank robbing, too." She refused to divulge names, however. "I know better than to talk," she whispered, as if the boards of her house had ears. "I know what happens to people who talk too much."

As a child, Lila said that she drove everyone crazy because all she wanted to do was laugh and have fun. In later years she turned to poetry. I never visited her without listening to a recitation of something she had just written. We would sit on her front porch and talk awhile, and suddenly, as if she had just thought of it, she would say, "I have a poem I'd like you to listen to. I think you might like it."

One afternoon, during a lull in our conversation, she said, "You know, I like you." (She spoke as if this realization had caught her by surprise.) "I don't know why I like you," she continued. "I just do. I know a lot of people who don't like you, or say they don't, but if they knew you I think they would. I don't see how they could help from it." After a long pause, she added, "I guess I like you because you seem to like my poems. You'll put up with them anyway."

Our Blue Heavens
by Lila Williams

IT'S A BUSY KIND OF WORLD all around us. Beans, corn, sugar cane's growing. The bees is busy making honey and the smell of a thousand flowers. The wind keeps blowing through our hair as we move down the stony path. It was like a streak of gold to us. God walks beside us and guides our way to the open space. With a little shack of a house, it is our fairy land to farm, born, and raise our children. As we sat on our little bit of heaven that we could never pull ourselves away, we could see the kind of love we held for each other. Every weakness and every strength as we sit near our little love nest, and we could hear the children play and the baby crying. The sun got low and the night was near, and I could hear the whippoorwill and the bobwhites calling their mates, smell the sweet perfume from the fields. As we looked up we could see the moon and the skies and the stars, all the beauty of the night spread out all over the world. When we grow old and weak we'll rest in our blue heavens.

"I've got part Devil in me," Lila admitted, "but I don't mean any harm. It's all in good fun."

She grew up with Mr. Pomp Meadows, who owned a general store in the nearby community of Colmesneil. "When he was a boy, Pomp was real prissy," Lila said. "He always had to be

Lila Williams

Lila Williams in her kitchen

dressed just so or he wasn't happy, but we sure had a lot of fun with him anyway because he scared easily. I'd put him in my car and drive fast over the dirt roads. Every time we hit a bump Pomp would squeal like a little pig."

A Most Eligible Bachelor

THROUGHOUT HIS LIFE, Pomp Meadows was a fastidious dresser, always starched and ironed with creases as sharp as blades. He was recognized as a ladies' man as well as a shrewd merchant, parsimonious to the extreme. As the story goes (and he told it on himself many times) he once sold a coffin to the parents of a thirteen-year-old girl who died suddenly. Although it was unlike him, he extended credit to the dead girl's father, allowing him to pay for the coffin over a period of months. Shortly before the funeral, Mr. Meadows realized that the father would never have the means to pay the debt so he repossessed the slightly used coffin, forcing the family to make other burial arrangements.

Mr. Meadows returned the casket to his store and was never able to sell it. He kept it on the gallery level with mattresses, rockers, and his father's wicker wheelchair.

When I was in high school my friends and I visited Mr. Meadows's store on our way to or from Lake Tejas, where we swam. We would, without fail, climb the stairs to the gallery and open the coffin, which was musty and slightly stained. After summoning our courage, we would try to lie inside it, but it was awfully narrow and only the smallest of us could squeeze down to size.

Many years later I moved to New York but returned to Texas

quite often to write. During that time I visited Mr. Meadows frequently because I wanted to buy the coffin and wheelchair. "Not for sale, *New York*," he would say. "Besides that, you can't afford my prices."

Half expecting him to change his mind I continued dropping in on him every chance I got. In the winter months I would find him sitting close to a wood-burning stove, and in the summer he was never far from an electric fan. Invariably, he was surrounded by a few solicitous ladies who had gotten themselves all dolled up just to keep him company. They fought to wait on him, to serve lunch, coffee, cold drinks, whatever his heart desired. And without a doubt, each lady spent a good portion of the day praying for a proposal, for Mr. Meadows, a confirmed and flirtatious old bachelor, was quite well off and considered to be a fine catch even at his age, about eighty years, I'd say.

"Here comes *New York*," he would announce to his lady friends when I entered the store. "I know what he wants. Nothing's on sale today, *New York*. I believe I'll keep that old casket and wheelchair for myself. I might need them if ever I get old or die."

A few years later, much to everyone's surprise, and possibly even his own, Mr. Meadows did die. Lynn Lennon and I were in the Big Thicket on a photographic excursion at the time. We heard that the store was being liquidated, and by the time we arrived there, everything had been sold except the casket. I asked Mr. Meadows's sister if she would sell it. "Why would anyone want a used coffin?" she asked. "To remember your brother by," I answered. When I offered twenty-five dollars her eyes opened wide. "I believe I better take it while I can get it," she said.

At last the coffin was mine.

For many years Mother kept it in her home and used it as a

coffee table. She said that it kept her drop-in visitors to a minimum. "Nobody stays very long anymore," she said happily. By then, her reclusive nature was in full bloom, and she relied on Pomp Meadows's coffin to scare everyone away. "Honey, you can't take that coffin with you when you go," she said, "for your crazy little mother needs it worse than you do."

After Mother's death, I shipped Mr. Meadows's coffin to New York and kept it on display in my apartment. Most of my friends were not unsettled by the coffin itself but by the strange rancid odor that emanated from it. The coffin had always had that odor, but it seemed to be growing stronger by the year. Finally, the smell permeated my entire apartment and was wafting into the hallway.

To rectify the situation I resorted to disinfectants of all kinds. I removed the gossamer and washed it, removed the straw padding from the bottom and threw it away. I sprayed and scrubbed and mothballed; I burned incense of all kinds, and still the coffin smelled of death. As a last resort, late one night my friend Dennis Donegan and I carried the coffin to the street and left it there. Then we dashed to the top of our building and leaned over the parapet to watch the pedestrians react to a velvet-covered coffin sitting on a Chelsea sidewalk. Some of them approached with curiosity, some ran, some lingered awhile, puzzling over what they had discovered. No one lifted the lid.

The next morning it was gone.

I regret having to tell this part of the story. Pomp Meadows's coffin contained many wonderful memories of sitting around the wood-burning stove in his store. It contained memories for many other people too, not just myself. Today, I can think of dozens of friends and acquaintances who would be glad to have that old coffin, odor or not. But I threw it away. I'm sorry now. I regret it. But that's what I did.

Of course there are those who will say, "So what? The story Pomp told on himself wasn't even true." But it doesn't matter to me whether it was true or not. It was a story, and a good one, and I among many others loved hearing it told again and again.

I think Lila Williams would agree with me in part, but she would see fit to add her say: "The story *was* true, every word of it."

Not long before her death she told me that Pomp always told the truth on himself, if no one else. "He sold the coffin and then repossessed it at the last minute," she said. "He not only enjoyed being mean, he enjoyed bragging about it too."

Roy Pate, one of Lila's contemporaries, said that Pomp Meadows should have given the casket to the poverty-stricken family. "That's what I would have done," he said. "They couldn't afford it, and they needed it worse than he did, but old Pomp was after every dime he could get his hands on. It made him sick to lose a penny, and it serves him right that he never made a nickel off that girl's coffin."

Roy Pate, Jethro Holmes, and the Dogwood Festival Parade

EACH SPRING Woodville goes all out to celebrate the blooming of the dogwoods. A pageant, written by a local citizen, is performed at night in an outdoor theater decorated with thousands of crepe paper flowers made by local ladies, students, and a few elderly gentlemen with nothing better to do. The pageant, commemorating some event in the history of Tyler County, takes place after the crowning of the Dogwood Queen, a high school senior who has competed in the categories of poise, beauty, intelligence, talent, and conversational skills.

On the afternoon of the pageant, a parade with many floats and marching bands winds its way through the Woodville streets. During my time, the high point of the day was Mr. Roy Pate, our grocer. He was always the last entry in the parade, and in Mother's opinion, "the only thing worth waiting for."

Each year Mr. Pate dressed up like a woman: Pistol Packing Mama, Annie Oakley, Pocahantas, or some old pioneer lady with a corncob pipe in her mouth and a proclivity for spitting. To the amusement of not everyone, he minced down the street blowing kisses and waving. For several years, Eva Gay furnished his shoes and helped him put together his costume, which was always outrageous. He seemed to be fond of tight skirts, high heels, and red hair. He fashioned his wigs from mops, yarn, twine, whatever was available, and he rarely shaved before painting his face with lipstick and rouge.

One year Mr. Pate dressed up like one of the rich high-and-mighty ladies of the town. He wore a blue sweater with a matching skirt, blue shoes, and bouffant wig. Everyone agreed that he impersonated this blue-haired matron with such perfection he must have robbed her closet. To exacerbate matters, he wore a sign on his back identifying the woman by name. Naturally, she did not enjoy seeing herself and complained bitterly. From then on Mr. Pate was not allowed to participate in the Dogwood parade. The conservative officials said he had gone too far, but for most of us, he could have gone even further. Without him, the parade has never been the same.

"Why did you pick on her?" I once asked Mr. Pate. But he would not give me a direct answer except to say:

"I have sold a lot of groceries in my day, and most of them on credit. Your mother, who didn't have much money, paid every cent she ever owed me. I cannot say the same for many of the rich people in this town."

Eventually, the Dogwood committee replaced Mr. Pate with another old-timer, Mr. Jethro Holmes, who sold firewood from a wagon pulled up and down the streets by two oxen named Tom and Jerry.

When he wasn't selling firewood he was in the top of a tree sawing off limbs. Even in his seventies, Jethro was not only the best tree surgeon in Woodville, he was the *only* tree surgeon in Woodville. As far as I know he did not go to school to learn this skill. Like everything else, he came by it naturally.

Jethro Holmes lived on the outskirts of town and society, was related to practically everyone in Tyler County, and like Roy Pate,

Roy Pate

was much loved by some and considered a nuisance by others. One thing was certain, he was a man of substance. He had a big heart, an open mind, and strong moral fiber.

During prohibition, Jethro made moonshine and sold it to the rich landowners in Tyler County. His still was located in a remote section of the Big Thicket, and parked all around it were getaway cars. He must have owned a dozen old wrecks that he used for delivering his bootleg. The law never knew what he would be driving next or what he would be wearing. He said that he changed hats as often as he changed cars, and for that reason he managed to avoid arrest for many years.

Jethro was a man of extraordinary compassion. He had no need for all the money he made from his whisky so he shared it freely with the poor families in the county. He practically ran a one-man welfare system, which collapsed after he was sent to Leavenworth for bootlegging. Without him, Tyler County was forced to start its own welfare department. Or so it is said. There's probably a good deal of truth to the statement.

At Leavenworth, Jethro was sentenced to manual labor. He assisted in the construction of various buildings both inside and outside the prison, and when his term was up he refused to leave because he was in the middle of a building project. He said that he had never in his life left a job unfinished and he wasn't going to break his record. After the building was completed, he left Leavenworth and returned to Tyler County, where he sold firewood from his wagon, doctored trees, and traveled with Tom and Jerry all over Texas.

Jethro and his oxen were invited to lead every other major parade in the state, but at home he was largely ignored. The committee members, who had the power of decision, were hesitant to solicit his participation in anything. After he became some-

Jethro Holmes

Jethro Holmes with Tom and Jerry

thing of a celebrity, he and his team of oxen were occasionally allowed to lead the Dogwood parade, but most of the time they were stuck at the very end.

"It doesn't look right for him to lead our parade," some committee person once said. "He did time in Leavenworth, you know."

LEAVENWORTH, Huntsville, and Rusk. During my day these places were spoken of frequently. Today it's about the same. Even though there is now a branch of the state penitentiary in Woodville, people are still saying:

"That boy's going to end up in Huntsville before it's all over with. They've got an electric chair over there that already has his name written all over it."

And if not that, this:

"The poor thing, she's in and out of Rusk and there's nothing the matter with her. She's perfectly healthy all over except for her mind."

Weary mothers may still be heard threatening their children:

"I'll send you to Rusk tonight if you don't behave yourself."

The East Texas town of Rusk continues to be famous for one thing: an insane asylum. Mother was always saying that she would end up there sooner or later. If we were invaded with too much company or visitors outstayed their welcome, Mother would usually run them off with her nervous energy.

"I've got the heebie-jeebies so bad I can't live," she would shout. "I'm on my way to Rusk for sure this time. Call them up and tell them I'm coming, but don't give them my real name. Let them think I'm somebody else. Then nobody will ever be able to find me, and I won't have to go on entertaining every idiot who knocks on my door."

Mother of Pearl

A FEW YEARS AGO, a shorter version of "The Widow Who Lived on the Hill" was published in *Texas,* the Sunday magazine printed in the *Houston Chronicle.* Not long thereafter, several people said to me, "I don't remember Pearl that way." For the most part they were people who had never lived with her. Those of us who had were mindful of her mercurial disposition. And so was she. Often she warned us of her bad days, or what she suspected might be one. "Honey," she would say, "your tired, old, worn-out mother's on pins and needles today. There are no if's and's or but's about it. Everybody better mind their p's and q's is all I can say." Hearing this, I would spread the word to Sissie or Butch or Frank's daughters. "Mother's on pins and needles again. Don't make any kind of noise. She's smoking one cigarette right after another."

On other occasions, she would become nervous or wild-eyed, and her voice would go on edge. "Darling, your old Mother's seeing flying colors today. I sure hope nobody comes over to visit." Again I would spread the word: "Beware."

Now and then, a member of the family would ask me to talk Mother into doing something or going somewhere, but if she was having a bad day, all I needed to say was, "Pins and needles," or "Flying colors." Those were perfectly acceptable answers, inside the family.

Outside the family, Mother was known as a mild-tempered woman who rarely expressed strong opinions unless she knew to whom she was speaking and thoroughly approved of the person, or unless she thought someone was cheating her; then she would speak her defense in such a way that forced her opponent to surrender with laughter, empathy, or just plain fear.

When I was about ten years old, I heard her scream at a mechanic for not repairing her car properly. It had snowed during the night. I had gotten up early and built a snowman on top of the car, which had just been repaired and paid for. "How can I go to town with that snowman on top of my car?" Mother ranted. "People already think I'm out of my mind." Actually, she couldn't wait to drive through town with the snowman. It was just the kind of thing that appealed to her. But when the car wouldn't start she lost her temper. "I have just paid a fortune to have this Ford fixed," she screamed. "Somebody's cheated me. Somebody's about to get a piece of my mind whether he wants it or not." After a neighbor gave us a push we creeped into town. Mother stopped in front of the body shop and got out of the car but refused to go inside the tin shed. "You come out here and talk to me, right now," she yelled. She stood in front of the car. I stood some distance behind it and watched with apprehension. The mechanic stepped outside his shop. I was trembling. The snowman was melting. Mother was flinging her arms around and screaming:

"For your information, I am nothing but a tired, old, contrary widow who lives four miles outside the city limits in a house that's falling down. I'm trying to raise my son and feed my mother on a veteran's pension, and that's not easy. I pay my own bills. I haul my own garbage. I vote like every other decent human being, but I'll be damned if I'm going to stand up here and pay you twice for work you have not done. Now I'm giving you one more chance to fix my car and that's all you'll get."

Her voice echoed off the tin walls of the body shop. I knew she was furious, almost over the edge, but I'm not so sure the mechanic realized this, for there was a deceiving wit mixed with Mother's wrath. I prayed that the man would not aggravate her further, and he didn't. Thankfully, he apologized and Mother calmed down, but she was obviously disappointed. She had her heart set on driving through town with the snowman on top of her car, but it melted before she had the pleasure of showing it off.

"You have such a sweet mother," the townspeople frequently said to me. And they were right. There was a genuine sweetness about her. She was gentle, kind, generous to a fault, and entertaining. But her personality did not stop there. Mother had a quick temper, a soft voice, and a sharp sense of humor that sometimes abandoned her to rage. Because she was reluctant to speak the undiluted contents of her mind she often relied on tones of irony to express her feelings, and therefore, most people did not realize the ferocious side of her personality, but it was certainly there. Lurking beneath her bright smile and laughter was something quite dark, and toward the end of her life the dark side seemed to be taking over. She could be laughing one minute and crying the next. At times she seemed to laugh and cry simultaneously.

Once she said to me: "Honey, if I couldn't laugh at your grandmother, I guess I'd kill her, and I might lose control and do it yet. Then I'll be sent to the pen, and my worries will be over. What

will you think of your old, cranky mother when she's living behind bars?"

THERE WAS a reclusive side to Mother's personality and
a strong gregarious side as well, although she was quick to admit
that she wasn't overly fond of human beings. When she became
restless at home she balanced herself out by taking odd jobs
around town, and when she got tired of working she simply quit
and that was that. For a while she worked in a five and dime, and
then a dry goods store and back to the five and dime, but she
preferred dry goods because she enjoyed selling yardage. She
never said why. Once, she landed a job in a flower shop, but after
two days she quit because she couldn't stand working with ribbons. "I can't tie a pretty bow to save my life," she said, and the
shop owner agreed with her.

Mother's favorite job was at a window factory. She worked on
an assembly line as a weather stripper and bragged about her
speed. "How can you go out there and work with such low class
people?" she was often asked. "All they are is niggers. Only the
scum of this county works at that factory."

"I don't care what you think," Mother said when she felt feisty,
"they're more *innersting* than anyone you'll meet up there at the
First Baptist Church." If she were tired she might choose to avoid
such a confrontation, in which case she would flash an insincere
smile and fume to herself, and later on to Grandmother or me.
The truth is, she liked her coworkers, especially the women who
weather stripped beside her. "Honey, you should hear some of the
things we talk about on the line," she would report to me. "You
would not believe what your ignorant mother is learning."

The major topic, of course, was sex. "I've learned more about sex than any tired worn-out widow needs to know," she announced to the line of weather strippers. "I haven't had a man in a hundred years, and have no intentions of getting me one, so I don't know why you all can't talk about something useful for a change. Think about me when you pick your topics of conversation."

"Pearl, we're always thinking about you," the weather strippers laughed. "Maybe we can find somebody who can improve your disposition."

"Don't try to fix me up with one of your Saturday night firecrackers," Mother said. "Too much agitation puts my nerves on edge."

Of all the weather strippers on the line, a black lady named Izella was one of Mother's favorites. Izella laughed at everything Mother said, and Mother laughed at everything Izella said. Naturally, they became fast friends. They even visited each other's homes, practically unheard of at the time because black people were still segregated from white people, had separate entrances to public bathrooms and restaurants, and were not allowed to enroll in white schools.

"On one hand Negroes are the happiest humans in the world," Mother was forever saying, "but on the other hand, they're not. They're just determined to make the best of hard times, and I'm just like them."

She enjoyed chatting with Izella, Beatrice, Etta, or various other black ladies who frequently dropped in for a visit. While the white countryside talked about Pearl Swift entertaining Negroes on her front porch, Mother remained unconcerned. She was accustomed to gossip by then. "People will talk about you no matter what you do," she said, "so you may as well go ahead and do whatever it is you want to do and enjoy yourself while you're doing it."

Of all Mother's black friends, I knew Beatrice Copes the best. Beatrice was a tall, large-boned woman who walked with the dignity of a queen in exile. She had a singing voice, an elaborate wardrobe, and a love of flowers and knickknacks. Mother gave her many a dust catcher, and that clinched the friendship. "I just love you since I met you, I'm so glad I did," Beatrice was forever saying.

By the time they got to know each other, Mother had become a champion gardener, and at home she usually dressed in old dirt-stained clothes. Beatrice, however, dressed to the nines. She was fond of big, starchy collars and costume jewelry displayed against dark fabric. She wore hats and scarves, shoes with buckles and flowers, and always carried an unusually small purse that made her look much bigger than she really was.

For hours on end Beatrice and my mother would sit on the porch like two prophets discussing things to come. Mother usually had a garden tool or fly swatter in hand, and Beatrice, all powdered and starched, carried something to fan her face, usually a hat, a newspaper, or a magazine. Chameleons lived on the porch and seemed to have no fear of the two ladies, and neither did the flies. "Beatrice," Mother would say, "hold still, you've got a fly on you. I'm about to get it." Then Beatrice would spring to her feet, "Don't be swatting on me. You'll dirty my dress." Mother would swat left and right like a crazy person. The chameleons would scurry away and Beatrice would scream, "Don't bother Mr. Fly."

Sooner or later they would settle down and Mother would broach one of the heavier topics of conversation, such as race relations. "Beatrice, do you think that Negro people and white people will ever get along?" How many times must she have asked this question, only to hear the same answer:

"Oh yes! There will come a time. A time when people will have no choice but to get along."

"And what will it take?"

"Maybe it will take something like Jesus Christ coming down off the cross. He'll have to walk the earth and heal all the wounds."

"And do you think that's going to happen?"

"Well, I have my doubts about it," Beatrice would sigh. "To tell you the truth. It might take something awful to happen, something we don't want to think about right now."

When they reached such a point in conversation, Mother's thoughts turned automatically to refreshments. She would serve cookies, sand tarts, or her famous orange cake with unbelievably strong coffee. Beatrice ate with small dainty bites and held her coffee cup with a curled little finger. She took her time, savoring each morsel, but Mother gobbled her cake rapidly and drank her coffee in three swallows. Soon the dishes would be pushed aside, and they would be cleaning out closets in search of forgotten knickknacks or digging up flowers for Beatrice to plant in her own yard.

Sometimes, I sat inside the house and listened to them. Their soft voices wafted through windows, walls, and closed doors.

"You are the nicest thing I ever saw," Beatrice once said. "How did you get to be so sweet anyway?"

213 / *Mother of Pearl*

"Oh, I'm mean as a snake, Beatrice," Mother answered.

And Beatrice replied, "Why do I believe I know you can be?"

MOTHER DID NOT go out of her way to befriend blacks, Indians, or Mexicans; she took a natural shine to them. She said that they had something to offer, something to say and a way of saying it. She also said that they had *a set of experiences.*

"Well, so have the rest of us," I once said to her.

"But not like theirs," Mother replied, as if I should have known this already. "They have had the kind of experiences that have made them the way they are, and that's something most white people will never know about."

Mother said that white people were judgmental and narrow-minded, and for the most part the ones she knew probably were. "I don't care what color someone is," she used to say, "if they're boring they're boring and your contrary old mother just hates to be bored worse than anything. And let me tell you something else: the more accepted you become the more boring you are because then you're just like everybody else."

"And what bores you most of all?"

"Ordinary, everyday people, honey!" She spoke as if shocked that I should need to ask the question. "Ordinary, everyday people just bore your mother to death. I can't get far enough away from them to save my life, and they're everywhere you step. You can't walk for them."

In tones of heavy irony she continued:

"Oh, I must be the most awful person in the world because I don't like anybody anymore and nobody likes me except every nigger at the window factory. Honey, your sweet little mother's nothing but a nigger at heart."

Once I heard her say, "Izella! I'm nothing but a weather-stripping nigger, just like you." And Izella laughed until tears rolled. "I always knew you were," she said, "I don't know why you're so long in finding it out."

I never heard Mother utter one word that an intelligent person would consider racist. Unfortunately, I cannot say the same about my grandmother. Shortly after we moved to Woodville a black lady, whose name I cannot recall, took an instant liking to Mother, and as result, she paid me a great deal of attention. Whenever we met up with her in town she commenced hugging and kissing me. In my dancing costume she might have thought I was a precious little girl. Who knows what she thought. Maybe she didn't even know herself. But there I would stand in my green skirt with toes turned out, and this old lady would nod to me and say to Mother, "Just look at *yours*. Just look at what you got here. I believe you got yourself *something* for sure." Then she would smother me with kisses and hugs. Snuff would drip from the corners of her mouth and run all over my face. Very calmly, Mother would wipe it off with a Kleenex and insist that I kiss the woman back. She also insisted that I say, "Yes ma'am," to her.

Somehow Grandmother heard about this. "Pearl," she said, "don't teach him to say 'Yes ma'am' to a nigger," and mother said, "But they are *peeeople!*" And Grandmother replied, "If they are, you're just like them. I don't know how I got stuck with a daughter like you."

Grandmother may not have liked Negroes, but she did like their cooking, especially the sandwiches made by Pat Brown. "Just because we happen to have the same last name," she told Mother, "is no reason for you to get it in your head that we're kin to the man, for we are not. The only thing good about Pat Brown is his sandwiches; the rest is no count." It was strange to me that Grandmother would eat a sandwich prepared by Pat Brown when most of the white people in the county testified that the meat was questionable. They said it was coon, possum, armadillo, and rodents of all kinds, even buzzards, lizards, and snakes. But what difference did that make to Grandmother? None. She begged for Pat Brown's sandwiches. Mother brought them home. And we ate them with relish.

Pat Brown lived only a few blocks from the courthouse square. A barbecue pit was in his yard, and he kept it going day and night. During the noon hour he walked the Woodville streets with a bucket of sandwiches. He wore a tall chef's hat and recited this jingle:

I've got barbecued chicken sandwiches, just made still hot.
There're so big and fat you wonder how I sell 'em like that.
They'll make you grit your teeth.
They'll make you curl your hair.
They'll make you feel like a millionaire.
You don't have to bite 'em.
All you have to do is waller 'em and swaller 'em.
Ground in a food chopper.
Barbecued.
Salt already.
Take fifteen cents and eat a chicken dinner.

Over the years, Mother must have bought hundreds of Pat's sandwiches. "I don't care what they're made of," she said, "they taste good, and that's the point, isn't it?

"Pearl, how do you know you're not eating skunk, or somebody's dead dog?" she was asked.

Pat Brown

"So what if I am," was her answer.

"Do you really mean that, Pearl?"

"If I said it, I guess I do. What do you think?"

Hardly anyone knew quite what to think. She was adored but certainly not understood, and people were always trying to analyze her. They wanted to know what went on inside her mind, the contents of her heart and soul. They wanted to know what she was all about, but hardly anyone ever found out because most of them had neither an appreciation for irony nor a grasp of the high level of humor and theatrics on which Mother operated.

But I understood her. And I can tell you what she was all about. Quite simply, she was about *sadness*. She was about transcending sadness with laughter. She was about the language, how she heard it, and how she spoke it. It was music. She was like a soprano singing Rossini. The second time through she embellished the line. She tried never to repeat herself, not even her embellishments, but of course, she did repeat herself, she repeated herself constantly; still she never stopped trying for something new the second time around. That's what she was all about.

Now and again she would say to me, "Honey, your old mother feels so sad today. She just wants to sit down and feel sad about herself and everybody else."

She did not say this in a way that solicited pity. She merely made a statement: "Honey, your old mother feels sad today. Today, is a very sad day." Her tone was matter of fact, as if making a comment about the weather: "Today it's going to rain." Or "Today the sun will shine."

Very few people understood her point of view; very few knew when to take her seriously and when to laugh. But those of us who were close to her knew that almost everything she said was serious, that even the hilarious statements were merely a cushion wrapped around a sad and tender heart.

I can't count the times I heard the same sad story about a winter coat that she dearly loved. She was thirteen years old. The place was Camp Ruby. The coat was red. The day her father bought it for her she backed up to a stove and burned a hole in the back of it. "Oh, I loved my coat," she would begin. "It was so beautiful and I ruined it. I have never been able to have anything fine in my life. I always ruin everything, no matter what. Oh honey, I loved my red coat more than anything." She would go on and on, repeating herself in a highly dramatic fashion, and sooner or later almost everyone would laugh, but she would shed a tear. She never quite got over that coat, and for those of us who realized this, the story was tragic—not far removed from her other great loss, my father. As far as I know, she did not grieve for him in public, not directly that is; she expressed her sadness in other ways.

There were a few tormented souls who seemed to have a keen sense of her. They sensed that she was *someone*, that she could help heal old wounds, that she was a balm. She had lived through grief and had emerged smiling, and for that reason the bereaved flocked to her door or called her on the telephone. They asked her all sorts of questions, hoping to find a clue into her personality, to gain a breath of relief or put an end to their mourning once and for all. Young or old, anyone who was troubled in one way or another found comfort when talking to her. "I am not a *psyche-therapy*," she would say. "I can't solve my own problems, but everybody thinks I can solve theirs and I can't." Still she listened to everyone in distress. Every mother and father who had lost a child, every widow or widower, every lost soul and forgotten love. "How do you get through it?" they would ask. "How do you stop grieving?" And to this mother would reply in a kind but very firm voice:

"You don't get over it; don't even expect to. You never stop grieving; don't even think you will. Just stay busy, put your mind on other things, and don't feel sorry for yourself; you don't have time for that."

"Do you think I should pray?" they sometimes asked.

Here Mother answered sharply, "You should do anything that makes you feel better, just as long as you don't hurt anybody while you're doing it." Then with devilment sparkling in her eyes she might add in a grave tone, "There's only one thing I ask: Please don't expect me to say a prayer for you or anybody else, because I'm so mean God himself won't have anything to do with me anymore, and you would burn in hell if I were to so much as mention your name in a prayer."

No matter what she said or how she said it, the bereaved sought her out, and to this day strangers will come up to me on the street and say, "When my wife died your mother was so sweet to me. She knew just what to say." "When my husband died, Pearl was an angel."

Although Mother was the first to admit that she didn't know why people wanted her opinions and advice, she never turned a deaf ear to someone in pain. With the face of an oracle she dispensed her own brand of wisdom, often to people she did not even know and whose problems were not clearly defined. "Oh Lord, honey," she frequently said. "The world is in a sad shape for sure. You should sit down and listen to some of the things I'm told. You would not believe your ears."

I have no idea what everyone told her, but I do know that she had a hard time keeping it all straight. Remembering who said what and when was not one of Mother's priorities. One night when I was in grade school a widower, still in mourning, called her up and told her that the words she had spoken to him the year before had given him so much comfort. He said that he needed to hear those words again. For a moment, Mother panicked. She hardly remembered the man. "Why, thank you so much for calling," she said in a tense but polite voice. "Tell me what I told you, and I'll try my best to say it again." The man told what she had said. She repeated what he told her, tacking on a few extra words, and when they hung up he was happy, at least for a while.

Because her personality had many colors and shades of colors, it is impossible to capture her in words alone. One would need to hear how she inflected those long, cadenced sentences, where she paused, where she shifted tones abruptly, where she suffered loss of confidence and fell into silence. One would need to see her eyes rolling heavenward on certain phrases and observe how she twitched her mouth around or flung her arms about when delivering the most serious pronouncements. Nothing about her was expected. There were always surprises. And nothing was too sacred or too serious for laughter. In her heart there was wit, sparkle, a touch of the absurd, as well as the prophet without honor. "Nobody believes a word I say," she would lament, knowing full well that everyone clung to her words. "Maybe I'll just stop talking. What do you think about that? Maybe I won't say anything to anybody ever again. What would happen if your silly, old, stupid mother never said another word? What would happen if your sweet Aunt Pearl never opened her mouth until the day she died?"

"It would be awful," we would tell her. "You can't stop talking. Not now."

Hearing us say this would thrill her, for she was, in her heart, an entertainer who entertained herself as well as others. She was a performer who often spoke of serious things facetiously, or facetious things with a seriousness that amused her, and although she often said she was like a bird without wings or a fish without a pond, she did not see herself as being out of step with the world; it was just the opposite—the world was out of step with her.

"Pearl," a matron of the town once said, "I've never known a white woman that Negroes and Mexicans love as much as you. Why is that, I wonder?"

"Well, the *Indins* love me too," Mother replied, offended that anyone should exclude the Indians from her list of admirers.

Mother boasted of our Indian blood, although many generations away, and wished that more of it had shown up on her. "Myrlie's got the Indian hair," she said. "And she doesn't even deserve it. She doesn't even want it. I wish it were mine and not hers."

Mother's hair was naturally curly and she hated it. She called it crawly hair and complained about it all the time. "All it does is crawl all over my head," she said. "It won't do anything it's supposed to." She wanted straight, blue-black hair. She wanted high cheekbones. She wanted to look like Dolores del Rio. She wanted to look like the Indian maiden on the cigar box. She wanted to look like Mary Beth, Eva Gay's first child, who was born with skin so dark she was almost purple. "We've got us another little Indin!" Mother sang when Mary Beth was born. "She's nothing but a little Indin, just like me." I'm not so sure Eva Gay enjoyed hearing this, but she heard it anyway. Mother was frantic with delight. Nothing could shut her up.

She held great respect for American Indians, especially the Alabama-Coushatta. We lived only a few miles from the reservation, and to hear Mother tell it we were related many times over to every Indian living there. The Alabama and Coushatta are twin tribes that speak a similar language and have always lived together. During the latter part of the eighteenth century, they came westward from the state of Alabama and settled in East Texas. Mother was crazy about them. She went to school with the Indians; they played basketball on the same team, and throughout her life they remained close. One of her favorite outings was to visit the reservation and talk to her old classmates. They generally started off with the same topic: their basketball tournaments.

"You used to step on my feet when we played ball," Mother would say. "That's why I can't hardly wear a shoe to this day. You have ruined my feet. I'm not going to claim kin to you anymore."

"You stepped on our feet too," the Indians reminded her, and from there the conversation would circle the basketball court for hours.

While the reservation was being developed into a tourist attraction, Mother made frequent visits to monitor the progress.

"Oh, I'm so proud of you Indins," she said. "I'm so proud of you Indins, I don't know what to do; you Indins are doing all the good, and I want you all to make a fortune so I can come out here and live with you for I am nothing but a tired, old, worn-out Indin just like the rest of you."

After the Indians became prosperous, fat, and diabetic, Mother was quick to tell them what she thought. "You Indins better watch yourselves," she said in a stern voice and without a trace of humor or irony. "You're getting too fat. You better lay off the sugar and give up the liquor before you kill yourselves off, and then I won't have no Indins to come out here and talk to."

"Pearl," someone once asked her. "Why does every minority that ever walked the earth like you?"

"Well not everybody likes me," she said. "The Jews in Battlestein's sure don't like me. They don't like me at all."

"Why?"

"Because I stare at them. Because I can't help myself either."

Battlestein's was one of Houston's big department stores. Shortly after my father's death we made several trips to Houston to consult a doctor about the removal of my birthmark. On arrival in the city, Mother would make a beeline to Battlestein's not to buy the merchandise but to admire the sales ladies. "Honey, have you ever seen so many beautiful Jews in your entire life?" she said to me. "Now they are what you call *mysteeris*. Now they are what you call *innersting* to look at."

I don't remember seeing any customers in Battlestein's. All I remember is my mother's nervous hand gripping mine, and the sight of all those salesladies standing behind glass cases with their hands folded. They were dressed in their finest: dark shoes, stockings, and costume jewelry sparkling against shiny black dresses. Their hair was slicked down, their eyelids tinted, their mouths and cheeks rouged. "Just look at them," Mother would exclaim. "They're painted to high heaven, and don't they look good? Honey, doesn't Battlestein's smell good? Don't you love coming here? Battlestein's is my kind of store. Don't you wish we had money to burn?"

Up and down the aisles we traveled, looking at everything and everyone but touching nothing. "Oh," Mother would sigh when she saw dresses that caught her fancy. "I sure do wish I could shrink my bones. If I could just think of a way to shrink my big old bones I'd be able to fit inside one of these pretty dresses."

Occasionally, a saleslady winked at me, and I wondered why I had been singled out for such an honor. I wondered what it meant to be winked at by such a person in such a place. Surely it meant something important, a blessing of some kind, for those salesladies stood like promises surrounded by scarves, purses and costume jewelry, watches and chains, dresses, blouses, and perfume. They were austere, removed from everyday life. Different. Who knows if they were all Jewish or not. Mother said they were because they worked in Battlestein's and Battlestein's was a Jewish name. She said they had to be Jewish because they had a certain style about them. They were composed. They were special. They were *big city*, fascinating to look at but very intimidating. "Smart," Mother said, "Jews are very smart people. They believe in education. They believe in a certain kind of food, and a certain way of doing things, but people get it in for them because they are *capable;* they can do anything they set their minds to. The world doesn't like you to be too smart or too good at doing things, don't ask me why."

I don't think Mother ever spoke to a single one of those salesladies, not even to nod hello. She was awestruck and a little frightened by their fine clothes and severe straight-up-and-down posture. And yet, she loved the store. She felt at home there, and she loved those silent saleswomen with their all-knowing eyes, their folded hands and varnished nails. The air surrounding them was cool and fragrant. And they were calm. Battlestein's was calm.

At last the war was over. The world was at peace. But the world was not really at peace, and the store was certainly not calm, it only seemed that way at first. It was filled with the *unspeakable*, and Mother was very much aware of this. "You can see it in their faces if you look," she said. "Sad, sad faces. A terrible thing has happened to the Jews over there." She nodded as if referring to the other side of the store. Puzzled, I looked in that direction.

"No, across the water," she said, irritated. She flung her arms around and pointed upward, but in no certain direction. "Over there where your father was. A terrible thing. That's why these women aren't smiling right now. They've lost everything, everyone. Nothing's left. Hardly anybody survived, not even your father. All it is is war, war, war and more war. The world is in a terrible fix. Humanity is in a terrible fix. No wonder these women look so sad."

Once I suggested that she might be able to make them feel better.

"Oh no," she said. "Your old mother's too stupid to talk to smart people. She wouldn't know what to say. She would make a pure fool of herself trying to get her words to come out right, and that's for sure."

To Mother, Battlestein's was a silent temple with a priestess behind each counter. They didn't talk to her, and she didn't talk to them, and she never made a single purchase. She just liked being there.

"Honey," she would say the moment we arrived in Houston, "let's go to Battlestein's. I bet they'll let us in."

I DON'T KNOW when Mother stopped painting her face and dressing up, or exactly why, but I suspect her change of appearance had to do with her forties wardrobe wearing thin, coupled with the burden of caring for her mother, along with a growing interest in gardening and the worry I caused her. She did not approve of my wanderlust, my desire to see new things. My restlessness disturbed her. Furthermore, she did not understand my insatiable curiosity. "It killed the cat," she said. "I believe you're just like Frank, always on the go, always looking for something better than what you've got. One of these days you'll have to settle down."

She was smitten with the *idea* of wanderlust but was miserable when she left home, especially if visiting relatives as far away as Pennsylvania. When it was just the two of us spending a day in Houston, Beaumont, or a few days in Galveston, she seemed to enjoy herself thoroughly, and although she longed to see Old Mexico she never allowed herself to go there. She did most of her traveling in her mind. "I'm nothing but a gypsy without a cart," she said. "What a fix to find yourself in."

Some of her homebody attitude can be traced to Grandmother's influence. She never wanted Mother and me to go anywhere, not even to a movie. She wanted us to stay at home where she could watch us. "That way," she said, "if something bad happens to you, I'll be the first to know about it."

If we went to the movies Grandmother panicked. She was terrified of being left alone, especially at night. Every noise frightened her. Every shadow was threatening. She imagined thieves, murderers, arsonists, ghosts, even rapists. Returning home after dark, we usually found her sitting in the living room with an open book in her lap and a cocked pistol in her hand. "Please don't leave me any more, Pearl," she begged. "I'm so scared way out here in the woods all by myself."

"If you didn't read all those murder magazines," Mother told her, "your imagination wouldn't run away with you."

Mother swore that we would never bring home another detective magazine or murder mystery because all they did was plant unhealthy seeds in Grandmother's overactive imagination. But Grandmother had a way of begging pitifully and relentlessly, and Mother or I always broke down and brought home whatever it took to keep her quiet. If it wasn't something to read it was sugar, both kinds.

"Thank you for my sugar, Pearl," she would say, meaning hard candy. "You know I don't have long to live anyway, so I might as well eat what I enjoy and be happy while I'm here. Just please don't move away and leave me all by myself. I don't have much time left. You can stay a little longer."

And so Mother stayed and stayed. And Grandmother lived and lived in spite of an enlarged heart, diabetes, and a steady supply of sugar.

Finally, her hour came. Twenty years after Grandfather's death, and only a few years before Frank's and Elton's, Grandmother took sick in the middle of the night and was taken to the hospital in an ambulance. As if in defiance of the fact that she had worried her life away and was certain that tragic death awaited us all, she died peacefully. Gradually her heart slowed down, and over a period of two days she resigned herself to the inevitable.

It was as simple as that. Her passing was quite ordinary and so was her will. She left an acre of land to each of her children and the house to Mother, but one of the most prized possessions, her wedding ring, which Grandfather had found on a Beaumont street, was up for grabs.

I was already living in New York and could not make it home

for the funeral, but Sissie took it upon herself to give me a full report. She said that while viewing Grandmother's body in the funeral home, Aunt Coleta said to Eva Gay, "Mama promised her wedding band to me so I'm going to take it now."

"No she did not," Eva Gay said. "Mama promised her ring to me. I know how Mama was. She would not have promised her ring to both of us. She wanted me to have it."

"Well take it then," Aunt Coleta said. "But when you're wearing it, I want you to remember who it belongs to." Eva Gay could not bring herself to remove the ring and neither could Aunt Coleta. "I can't touch her to take it off," she cried, "for last night I dreamed I pulled Mama's finger clean off her hand trying to get it."

The ring was buried with Grandmother, and for many years thereafter, neither sister was very happy about it. Eva Gay retaliated, however, but not against Coleta. If she couldn't have the ring, she intended to have Grandfather Gay's branding iron with letters G-A-Y. Mother was using it as a flower bed decoration, and Eva Gay pulled it up and took it home. The truth is, I wanted the branding iron myself, but Mother pleaded with me to keep my mouth shut. "Whatever you do," she said, "don't get my baby sister stirred up."

Mother not only inherited the house and an acre of land but all the solitude she dreamed of. "You can't live out there all by yourself, Pearl." Almost everyone told her this. "Maybe we can find someone to live with you. A nice elderly person to keep you company."

"I don't want any more old people around me, thank you," Mother answered. "What makes you think I want to take care of somebody, anyway?"

To me she said:

"I am sick to death of old people and people who want me to take care of old people; I've been around old people all my life, and as far as I'm concerned they can take care of themselves the best way they can or go find somebody else to put up with them; I'm not the one."

"What will you do way out there all by yourself, Pearl?" she was often asked. Her reply was:

"Plenty."

By then, all she wanted to do was sit in her yard, drink strong coffee, smoke cigarettes, garden, and bake. She was known for her orange cake, a recipe Aunt Bessie clipped out of a magazine and Mother perfected.

During Dogwood Festival preparations she always baked an orange cake for the ladies who made paper flowers at the First Christian Church. She would cut paper-thin slices and lay them out on a pretty plate. "Pearl," the flower makers exclaimed. "What kind of cake is this? Bring thicker slices next time."

"They're as thick as they'll get," Mother said happily. "I've got to save some for myself, you know."

Occasionally, someone asked her to bake an orange cake for a special occasion, but with one exception, Mother refused to go to all the trouble. "I'm not in the baking business," she replied. "I've got other things to think about."

The one person Mother never refused was Mrs. Josiah Wheat, whose husband, the county judge, had created the Dogwood Festival. Mother would do anything for Mrs. Wheat, even bake an orange cake to order. "Old Lady Wheat is a good old soul," Mother said. "She's common as an old shoe. Everybody knows she was born on the river bottom, and she knows it too; she came from nothing but nothing, and after she married *somebody* and turned into *something* it never went to her head; isn't that the way to be?"

PEARL'S ORANGE CAKE

1 cup of butter
2 cups of sugar
1 teaspoon soda mixed in 1 ⅓ cups of buttermilk
4 cups of flour
1 tablespoon grated orange rind
4 eggs slightly beaten
1 cup of nuts

Mother used hickory nuts from the trees in our yard to give the cake a taste of the earth. Of course, hickory nuts are difficult to find in a store. Walnuts will do but are not quite right.

Combine butter, sugar, eggs, and orange rind. Add a little buttermilk-soda mixture and stir. Then add a little flour and combine. Repeat until there is no more flour or buttermilk left and then fold in the flour-dusted nuts. Pour into a cake ring and bake for 1 hour at 350 degrees.

ORANGE CAKE GLAZE

2 cups sugar
1 cup fresh orange juice
1 teaspoon fresh lemon juice
2 teaspoons grated orange rind

Combine in a saucepan. Cook slowly until sugar dissolves and mixture thickens slightly. Then pour over hot cake. It will gradually absorb the mixture. Allow to cool before removing cake from pan. It's good the day it's baked, but much better if aged several days.

This is the basic recipe. What Mother might have done to dress it up a bit, I'm not sure. At the last moment she might have added a shot of liquor to the glaze. I do recall her saying, "I've got to go to the county line to get me a little bottle of something to bake with." I assumed the little bottle of something was rum or bourbon. This would certainly explain why she sometimes aged an orange cake for a week before cutting it. But when I add liquor to the glaze, it is tasty for sure, but not Mother's touch. Also, she never skimped on anything. Teaspoons and tablespoons were always heaping, and she believed in doing a little more, never a little less, particularly when grating orange rind or chopping nuts. (As much as a half a cup of orange rind often went into the glaze.)

The cake, the way Mother made it, was unspeakably delicious and beautiful as well. But she made it even more delicious by parceling it out in tiny slivers. "If I give them too much," she said, "they won't like it as well, but if I'm stingy with my slices, they'll want more. Their mouths will water. They'll think they've just eaten something that's out of this world."

After baking an orange cake she would leave it in the center of her kitchen table for all who dropped in to admire. "Come look at my cake," she would beg. "It really turned out this time."

"Oh, Pearl!" her visitors exclaimed. "When are you going to cut it?"

"When *I* get ready to," Mother would answer with a sly but wicked smile.

MOTHER GARDENED the same way she baked. Completely disregarding instructions and proper planting seasons, she planted and transplanted during any time of the year, including the heat of summer, and she rarely killed a plant. Anyone who asked her for a cutting received it. Anyone who wanted a bush or a shrub got the one they wanted.

"Pearl Swift is the most free-hearted thing," the ladies in town said. "If you see anything growing in her yard and you want it, you can just pull it up, practically without even asking."

"There's nothing free-hearted about me," Mother argued. "If I don't get rid of some of these flowers and bushes, I'll be living in a jungle before long."

Wild grapes took over the back yard. Lilies of all kinds marched around the house, as did hydrangeas, old maids, wood fern, and monkey grass, daisies, bridal wreath, pansies, phlox, and larkspur. Mimosas sprouted up everywhere and were allowed to grow without much pruning. Fig trees, large and small, were scattered about as were hickories and pines. In the front yard there was a cedar, a magnolia, a catalpa, various kinds of oaks, and a sweet gum. Just outside her kitchen door was an Asian pear and a chick-a-pen.

After Grandmother's death, pots that once contained hot peppers were taken out and replanted with portulaca, verbena, hen and biddy, Mexican gem, and donkey tail. Mother had them hanging or sitting on the porches, on tables and chairs, or simply arranged on the lawn. She was crazy for succulents because they did not demand her everlasting attention, and she was very fond of any kind of flowering tree and creeping vine, especially a wisteria.

About the only flower she did not care for was the gladiola. It reminded her of funeral sprays, and funeral sprays reminded her of death. At the same time she was passionate for anything that bloomed at night.

Surprisingly, there were always a few dead spots in Mother's yard, not necessarily spots where something had died, but spots where not much of anything, not even a succulent, would grow. She had a particularly hard time with two back corners, and finally she gave up on them, allowing whatever wanted to grow there to have its way. One of the corners ended up being rather bare, but the other became infested with weeds and copperheads. The back yard was never as beautiful as the sides and front, but Mother said that it wasn't supposed to be.

All in all, the yard was quite orderly but did not give the impression of being planned in advance due to the volunteers that sprouted up each year. And although it was certainly overgrown, it was not a jungle by any means, but it was filled with woodland animals. Mother insisted on feeding anything that wandered up.

She fed raccoons on her kitchen porch, and the possums that found their way to a large fig tree growing next to her bedroom window were allowed to eat their fill even though their loud smacking kept her awake at night. She had a soft spot for deer and flying squirrels and was fascinated by the bats that invaded our summer skies. Any bird that sang at night intrigued her, and if an owl chose to show its face during the light of day, she was sure it was for some important reason. Throughout the year she fed songbirds table scraps and store-bought seeds, and she spoke to them as if they were children. "You redbirds better come get this food before something beats you to it," she would shout. "And you blue jays sure better behave yourselves today. That's what I have to say."

It was the same with the chameleons. They were everywhere, and she loved them. She enjoyed watching them catch flies, change colors, or show their money (their bright red throats).

She was not too fond of dogs, however, because they dug up her flowers, and she hated red wasps, bumblebees, yellow jackets, and snakes. The yard was overrun with snakes, many of them poisonous, and Mother was careful where she stepped. She allowed the non-poisonous snakes to live because they kept the rats down, but if she came upon a poisonous one she would run for the grubbing hoe and chop the serpent into dozens of tiny pieces. She would chop and chop, practically digging a hole to China. Then she would rake what was left of the snake out of the dirt and burn it on a pile of leaves so its friends and relatives would catch the scent and stay away. But that never worked, and she was constantly involved with snake killing.

"How do you know when a snake is dead, Aunt Pearl?"

"You never can tell about a snake," Mother said. "They'll come back to life on you if you don't watch out. It's best to chop them up fine."

Once a copperhead bit her on the ankle, and she was sick for a long time. "Maybe if I hadn't killed so many," she said, "that snake wouldn't have made me so sick, maybe it wouldn't have even bitten me. I must be a mean old thing for something like this to happen to me, but it's too late to change." She continued killing every poisonous snake she found.

"I kill them, but I don't eat them," she said. "I'm not like they are way out West where they'll eat rattlesnake and say it's better than fried chicken. I'm not like Old Lady Durham either."

Alma Durham was Great-Aunt Rachel's sister-in-law.

She lived up the road from us and ate songbirds. To hear her talk she practically lived on them. Once she tried to give Mother a little handmade bird trap that was constructed of sticks and twigs all tied together, but Mother refused to take it. Mrs. Durham, on the other hand, trapped every bird she could. She either fed them to her hungry cats or enjoyed them herself, fried so crisp she could eat bones and all. "The sweeter they sing, the better they taste," she once told my mother. "You could cut down on your grocery bill, if you wanted to, and you'd never have to buy special food for all your cats."

"If my cats want to eat a bird," Mother said, "they can catch it themselves. That Old Lady Durham will eat anything if she thinks it'll taste good and I just can't stand to set foot in her yard. Everywhere you step all you see is feathers, redbird feathers, blue jay feathers, mockingbird feathers. I don't know how anybody could eat anything that knows how to sing. A chicken is different. A chicken has no voice. But could you, could you honestly eat a redbird if you knew what you were eating? I don't believe I even have a cat that could stomach a songbird."

Mother always had domestic pets, as well as wild ones that came in from the woods for a feed. Most of the pets were inherited from me: a Siamese cat, a Persian cat, and an Amazon parrot named Gulliver. The parrot lived in the pear tree during the summer, and in the winter he perched on top of doors and chairs and chewed everything to splinters. Mother loved that old parrot, in spite of the fact that he was messy, contrary, and demanded attention. "You're going to chew the house down," she would scream. "And then where will I go? What will I do? I'm too mean for anybody to take me in after I'm homeless." She was always begging Gulliver to fly away and never come back, but of course, he

Alma Durham

stayed. No animal, wild or tame, wanted to leave after taking up with Mother.

At one time she had as many as eighteen cats. People left them in her yard in the dead of night, and she took care of them as best she could. "My cats are as wild as billy goats," she said. "I don't know what I'm going to do with so many. They'll run me crazy before long."

Soon sand fleas found their way into her house, and to rid herself of them she resorted to the garden hose, but that did very little good. The battle with fleas continued until she claimed to have lost her mind and half her blood from scratching. "I'm nothing but a weary, old, penniless widow," she told everyone in her path. "I can hardly afford to put food on my table much less feed all these wild cats, and they're every one eaten up with fleas. Now I'm covered with bites, my nerves are bad, my floors are rotting to the ground, and I don't know what in hell I'm going to do next."

"Pearl Swift says the funniest things," everyone said. "How can she think of it all?"

"I am on pins and needles over these damn cats," Mother shouted and everyone laughed as if she were just putting on.

Suddenly all the cats disappeared. All at once, they were gone. "Oh, I don't believe I know what happened to them," Mother said, rolling her eyes around. "I guess they got tired of me and ran off."

A few years later, I found out what happened to all the cats. Mother and I were walking down a dirt road when she suddenly stopped and clutched her heart. "Oh, honey," she said. "I need to smoke me a cigarette right now."

"Why right now?" I asked.

"I don't like this walk as much as I used to," she said.

"Why?" I asked again.

Smoking nervously, she replied:

"Every time I come to this spot in the road my conscience starts hurting me bad because right over there is where I buried eighteen cats that were eating me out of house and home."

"Mother! Did you bury them alive?"

"Don't ask me that!" She raised her voice and flung her arms every which way. "I can't even stand to think about it."

I assume the answer would have been "yes."

BETWEEN 1972 and 1976, Grandmother died, Frank died, and Elton died. Then on July 27, 1978, on the day my first novel was officially published, Mother died in Sissie's home. She would have been fifty-nine that coming November. It is possible that she had known for five to seven years that she was terminally ill but kept it to herself. During that time she would clutch her heart and say, "Darling, I don't believe your old mother has long to live." There wasn't the slightest hint of irony in her voice. I knew she was speaking from her heart.

Many times I said, "Maybe you should go for an examination." (I don't think Mother had ever had a physical examination in her life, until the very last.)

"No!" she replied adamantly. "Your ugly old mother doesn't want a nasty-minded doctor putting his hands all over her."

A distant cousin visited her one day and found her on the floor, doubled over with pain. Still, she would not visit a doctor, and no one wanted to force her. Throughout her life, I remember her saying, "If anything ever gets the matter with me, I don't want to be cut on. After they open you up and the outside air gets inside, you can go overnight." She was convinced of this and refused to visit a doctor until the pain was unbearable, and although she finally submitted to surgery, by then it was too late.

About two o'clock on the morning of July 27, 1978, I woke up knowing that someone was in my apartment. I was living on lower Second Avenue in New York. I sat up in bed. A cloudy figure was standing before me. At first I did not recognize my mother's apparition. Her cheeks were puffy, almost swollen, and her dress was an indistinguishable murky substance. I was not at all afraid. The image faded. Then I drifted back to sleep. A few minutes later, the telephone rang. I was still sitting up in bed. Butch told me that Mother had just died.

"She was here," I said. "A few minutes ago, she was standing before my bed."

Mother had been recovering from surgery. She had varicose veins and was supposed to wear support hose. The doctor had instructed her to wear the stockings at all times or else a blood clot in a swollen vein might break away and race to her heart, causing instant death. She hated those support hose and certainly didn't like what was happening to her any better. The night she died she took the stockings off and threw them on the floor.

"I'm not wearing these damn things any more," she told Sissie.

"Pearl," Sissie said, "You know what the doctor told you."

"I know," Mother replied.

In the middle of the night she got out of bed, sat down in her chair and died instantly, the way she wanted.

When I arrived home, Sissie insisted that I stay with her, but I refused. I preferred to spend the night in Mother's house. That, I thought, was a way of facing her death and dealing with it. I arrived home after dark and found the house exactly as Mother had left it. A nightgown was hanging on a bedpost. Her favorite coffee cup was crusty with sugar. A newspaper was opened to the horoscope page, and her broom was in the middle of the kitchen floor where she had dropped it. I opened the outside door. A raccoon on the porch was begging to be fed. I gave it some bread and then turned on every light in the house.

While I was in one of the back rooms, I heard a woman's piercing voice, "Eddie, Eddie, my darling, you've come home. You've come home." My heart almost stopped. From the hallway I could see the front door. A woman's pale face was slightly visible through the screen. She kept singing in a high voice, "You've come home. You've come home."

Suddenly, Sister Louise danced into the room like a sunburst. "*Ishee-ma-*HA," she sang. "*Ishee-ma-Ha-ya-ma-*HA, *Lord Jesus.*" Behind her came Sister Flowers dancing on tiptoes. With her arms in the air and her palms turned upward, she threw back her head and surrendered to the Pentecostal spirit.

"Bless this house, Lord," Sister Louise shouted. "Take our dear Pearl into your bosom." While dancing wildly about, she slapped the Holy Spirit on my head, and Sister Flowers did likewise. "Lord bless this house," she shouted, "and hold our precious Pearl close to you."

This went on for quite some time until Louise finally looked up and *saw* me as if for the first time.

"Oh," she said, emerging from rapture. "We frightened you, didn't we? Lord heal our dear friend, don't let him be afraid of the dark."

I begged the two women to leave me alone. Reluctantly they left, and I have never seen either of them since.

MOTHER was a member of the First Baptist Church, although she rarely attended a service and had stopped going to Sunday school altogether. Therefore, choosing a minister to speak at her funeral was not easy. She had little use for organized religion, and if there was anything she hated worse than going to church it was going to Sunday school with the Wisteria Women. (At that time, most of the ladies' Sunday school classes were named for flowers.) One by one, the Wisteria Women had twisted Mother's arm to join them in class or attend their parties, which they called *socials*. "Please bake an orange cake and come be with us," they begged. But Mother refused them time and again. Finally she told her Sunday school teacher that she would occasionally attend class but on two conditions: "Do not call on me to read aloud, and do not call on me to pray aloud." The Sunday school teacher made this promise, and after a few Sundays, she called on Mother to deliver the closing prayer. Mother sat there with her teeth clinched, and did not utter a word.

"The Lord told me to call on you, Pearl." That was the Sunday school teacher's excuse, but Mother did not accept it.

"There's not a wistery woman in that class you can trust," she said. "I don't like any of them pretty good! And I'll be damned if I'll ever go back."

Although she had no respect for the Wisteria Women, she did have sympathy for the pastor of the Baptist church. She said that she believed he might be the only real Christian among a house filled with hypocrites and downright liars. "Brother Pastor," she said, "has one hell of a job cut out for him."

With that in mind, I chose the Baptist minister to preach mother's funeral. Had it been my decision alone, I would not have attempted a traditional service, but that would have upset members of the family, and although the Baptist minister was not acceptable all the way around, he was, at least, one step in the right direction.

There was controversy, however. It arose over Mother's coffin. Throughout her life she said to me: "Hon, don't spend money on me when I die. Just put me in a pine box and dump me in a ditch." Sometimes she would say, "Darling, when I die, don't spend your hard-earned money on me. Just put me in a paper sack and throw me in the river." Keeping all this in mind, I ordered Mother's coffin over the telephone. "Just a very simple pine casket," I said. "Very simple. Very pretty." And that it was. Those who knew her well said, "That's exactly what Pearl wanted." But those who did not hissed: "That casket will rot in less than a year."

That I allowed the coffin to remain open at the funeral home but requested that it be closed during the service was another point of contention, and because I refused to view Mother's body at all, even from a distance, someone was always whispering in my ear, "Eddie Jr., don't you think you ought to go look at your mother now?"

"She appeared to me the night she died, and that's how I'll remember her." I don't know how many times I said this. Even Sissie, who had taken care of Mother until the very last, came under attack for not attending the service. "I just can't go to another funeral," she cried. "Watching them die is hard enough. I've already done my part."

But after all was said and done, it was the pastor who angered everyone the most. During the funeral sermon, he stared at

Butch, a real estate salesman, and said, "I don't care how many pieces of real estate you sell, that will not take you to heaven." Then he looked straight at me and said, "I don't care how many books you write, they will not transport you into the Kingdom of God."

While he was preaching Mother's funeral, the Texas critics were reviewing my first novel about a boy more comfortable in dresses than pants. Although my mother did not entirely approve of the life I had chosen, she was proud of that book. It made her laugh out loud, and if there was one thing she loved, it was laughing. "Honey," she said, "let me give you some advice. You'll never get anywhere writing about yourself. You'll have to write about this tired, old, worn-out widow in order to be a success."

After her burial, I was told that people were saying:

"You know that book killed Pearl."

"You know, he'll have to pay for that."

By then I was already accustomed to the babbling of the small-minded and was far more amused than angered. Mother had always said to me:

"Honey, people will get right up in your face and say anything they want to. But only if you let them."

And once again, she was right.

Grandfather's Finger

E VERYONE WANTS TO KNOW what has happened to Grandfather's finger. "Do you still have it?" I am constantly asked this question.

The answer is, "No, I gave it away."

A few years ago Sissie said to me, "Eddie Jr., Joe Mur sure does want that ole finger when you get ready to do something with it."

At that time her son was a senior in high school. He wanted to go to college but was having a hard time keeping his grades high. I promised Sissie that I would will the finger to him, but a few months later, when we were talking on the telephone, she told me that Joe was having trouble with his college entrance examinations. "He just needs encouragement," she said.

At that time I sent the finger back to Texas with a little note attached:

"Joe Mur, this is yours."

I wasn't ready to give the finger up, but I figured that my cousin needed it more than I did. Maybe it will give him the incentive to study. That was my thinking at the time, and apparently it worked.

All because of Grandfather's finger?

Of course, Grandfather always believed in getting a good education, no matter how much it cost.

My grandfather's finger